Animal Welfare

ISSUES
(formerly Issues for the Nineties)

Volume 3

Editor

Craig Donnellan

Independence
Educational Publishers
Cambridge

First published by Independence
PO Box 295
Cambridge CB1 3XP
England

British Library Cataloguing in Publication Data
Animal Welfare – (Issues Series)
I. Donnellan, Craig II. Series
179.3

ISBN 1 86168 079 1

Printed in Great Britain
City Print Ltd
Milton Keynes

Typeset by
Claire Boyd

Cover
The illustration on the front cover is by
Pumpkin House.

CONTENTS

Chapter One: Animal Research

Chapter Two: Hunting

Chapter Three: Animal Cruelty

Introduction

Animal Welfare is the third volume in the series: **Issues**. The aim of this series is to offer up-to-date information about important issues in our world.

Animal Welfare looks at animal research, hunting and animal cruelty.

The information comes from a wide variety of sources and includes:
Government reports and statistics
Newspaper reports and features
Magazine articles and surveys
Literature from lobby groups
and charitable organisations.

It is hoped that, as you read about the many aspects of the issues explored in this book, you will critically evaluate the information presented. It is important that you decide whether you are being presented with facts or opinions. Does the writer give a biased or an unbiased report? If an opinion is being expressed, do you agree with the writer?

Animal Welfare offers a useful starting-point for those who need convenient access to information about the many issues involved. However, it is only a starting-point. At the back of the book is a list of organisations which you may want to contact for further information.

*****

Animal experimentation

Information from the Christian Medical Fellowship (CMF)

Using animals to advance scientific knowledge, understand disease, develop new medicines, or test the safety of chemicals is highly controversial. At one extreme people think that there are no moral problems, while at the other, some people justify violence to protect animals. A recent survey found that most young people in the UK were uneasy about animal experiments, or thought that they should be banned.

Animal experimentation is a huge industry. Each year in the UK scientists use almost 3 million animals. While the majority are rats and mice, one per cent are rabbits and 0.1 per cent are monkeys.

Most animals are used to help develop and test drugs for treating human diseases, although about 17,000 animals are used each year in the safety testing of food additives and household cleaning products. The number involved in these tests is falling rapidly.

However, in addition to these uses, the Ministry of Defence uses animals in weapons testing, but publishes little information about numbers or species involved.

While some of the traditional ways that animals have been used in experiments are on the decline, new areas are opening up. Experiments that involve genetic engineering are using increasing numbers of animals. In some of these, human genes are introduced into an animal. These transgenic animals may then develop diseases that are very similar to those of humans.

By studying the way that the disease affects these transgenic animals, scientists can discover how human diseases are caused. They are then in a better position to develop new treatments for human sufferers of the condition.

Pharmaceutical companies and research laboratories are also using transgenic animals to produce drugs. One of the first examples of this is a sheep that produces milk containing a protein called human alpha-1-antitrypsin. Doctors need this protein if they are going to be able to treat patients with a particular type of fatal liver disease.

Researchers have also cloned animals, the most famous being Dolly the sheep. Clones are exact copies of the parent animal in a method that is the genetic equivalent of photocopying. Combining transgenic technology and cloning may enable scientists to produce hundreds of identical animals that can make human proteins to treat human disease.

Experiments and the law

In the UK animal experiments are regulated by an Act of Parliament.[1] This act controls 'any experiment or other scientific procedure applied to a protected animal which may have the effect of causing pain, suffering, distress or lasting harm'. Protected animals are mammals, birds, reptiles, fish and amphibians.

All experiments must be performed in a laboratory that has received a Certificate from the Home Office indicating that it meets required standards.

On top of this, any individual involved in the experiments must have a Personal Licence. This licence should only be given to people who are competent to perform each stage of the experiment. For example, they may need to be able to give anaesthetic in a way that makes the animal free from pain.

Finally, the proposed experiments have to be approved and need to be conducted under the authority of a Project Licence.

An independent committee assesses each application and decides if the potential benefit outweighs any suffering. It also investigates whether the experiment could be done without using animals.

As part of its assessment, the committee grades the degree of animal suffering that will take place. Experiments are grouped into those in which the animal suffers little, for example, being painlessly killed before its tissues are analysed; those with a moderate degree of suffering, where for example the animal has a course of injections; and experiments in which animal suffering is severe.

About five per cent of approved applications involve severe suffering. Even then, limits are set for the permissible level of suffering in any experiment. In cancer research, animals have to be killed painlessly when the lumps of cancer cells in the animal get beyond a certain size.

Any industrial company wanting to use animals to test chemicals, household products and cosmetics has to follow very similar procedures. The few companies that still had licences for testing cosmetics have voluntarily relinquished them, so testing cosmetics on animals is now a thing of the past in Britain.

The law does not cover experiments on invertebrates, so insects and worms are not given legal protection. Some of the most important recent advances in biology relevant to medicine have come from studies of fruit flies and microscopic worms. The genes that are important in the normal development of flies from eggs and larvae are similar to genes in humans that cause diseases such as cancer. Scientists can produce transgenic flies in a fraction of the time and at a fraction of the cost of making transgenic mice. Consequently, they will be increasingly used in medical research.

Moral issues

Can we ever justify animal suffering?

People come to very different conclusions if the suffering is caused in order to help humans.

The answer depends on how we view animals and humans. There are three conflicting contemporary views.

The Animal Liberation Movement[2] sees humans as just one of many animal species, with no grounds to claim to be superior over any other kind of animal. By that argument, animal experiments are just as offensive as racism or sexism. It is purely cruel treatment driven by prejudice.

The opposing view is that humans own animals, which are intrinsically inferior. Animals have value because they are useful to humans. There are no limits to what humans can do to animals in the interests of human welfare or profit.

You could argue that anyone who is prepared to allow the destruction of animals by industrial pollution, as well as some of the 'factory farming' practices of modern agriculture, also holds this view.

A third view derives from the Christian perspective. This holds that despite many biological similarities between humans and animals, humans are uniquely and supremely valuable. Many people find that there are clear distinctions between humans and animals, for example being able to appreciate beauty and having a conscience about what is right and wrong.

In the language of Genesis, the first book of the Bible, while all people are 'made in the image of God',[3] animals are not. God values human beings so highly because he can have a personal relationship with them. This puts the value of humans above all animals. However, God brought all life into being, both animal and human.

The Bible goes on to say that we have a duty to care for the world, including the animals in it. Animals are not ours to do with as we like. People are seen as caretakers of the natural world.

We are made to live in caring relationships with God, each other and the natural world. We are ultimately answerable to God who owns everything.

Are all animals equally valuable?

Many people feel uncomfortable about experiments involving the 'higher' animals like chimpanzees. These animals have highly developed intelligence and language skills and display emotional behaviour that seems similar to humans. In the same way, people are disturbed by the thought of cats, dogs and rabbits being used in experiments. Animals which are less intelligent or attractive and which are not kept as pets arouse less concern.

It is possible that chimps suffer in ways that lower animals such as mice do not. These higher order animals may experience more emotional types of pain, such as fear or anxiety, during experiments. It is impossible to know if the insects and worms used in experiments can suffer, as their nervous systems are so simple that scientists doubt whether they can even feel pain.

Because we will never know whether different animals can experience suffering, it may seem right always to use a simpler animal where possible – a fly or a tadpole instead of a mouse. In addition, it seems reasonable to provide each species with conditions that are likely to minimise stress.

The experiments

If we have responsibilities to both humans and animals, we have to face

ITS ALL RIGHT – ITS RAT FUR

the moral dilemmas of animal experimentation. The problem is that animal experiments used to help care for people and alleviate human suffering clash with our duty to care for animals.

We may decide that carrying out a particular experiment is the lesser of two evils, whilst another involves animal suffering that cannot be justified. We have to ask searching questions of the experimenters who want to experiment on animals.

Must the experiment cause suffering?

In some cases there is no way of preventing all suffering. However, all effort should be taken and the experiment designed to minimise this.

Can the experiment give a clear answer?

All experiments should be designed so that they are capable of giving useful results. If this has not happened, the experiment is neither scientifically nor morally acceptable.

Is the experiment finding new data?

Until recently, it was common practice to use live animals in teaching some science classes like physiology in universities. These 'experiments' seem difficult to justify with the availability of modern teaching methods.

Can experiments for cosmetics and food additives be justified?

If animal suffering is seen as wrong we may seriously question its use for testing the safety of commercial products that we might consider non-essential. Do we need new chemicals in food or cosmetics enough to justify the animal suffering involved in their safety testing?

While most people use cosmetics to satisfy ideas of fashion, how about those who have facial scars and need cosmetics so that they feel socially acceptable? Is commercial gain something that can outweigh animal suffering?

If we reject animal experiments for commercial reasons, we also need to think about the treatment of the millions of animals in some modern intensive systems of farming.

Do we need to test all new medicines?

Animal rights campaigners do not believe that we need all of the drugs developed by drugs companies and tested on animals. However, while currently available drugs can cure some diseases, there are few or no treatments for some medical conditions, such as mental illness and many common cancers.

Before new drugs are tested on patients, the law requires they are tested on animals.

Although an increasing number of drugs are being designed to have specific effects, animal testing sometimes reveals unexpected side-effects that prohibit their use in humans. Animal experiments also help doctors decide what is likely to be a safe dose for humans. Given the degree of human suffering from diseases for which we have no effective treatment, many think drug testing on animals is justified.

Can we justify experiments on animals that have no obvious benefit to human health?

Scientists are very keen to protect what they see as their right to carry out experiments on animals that have no direct or immediate relevance to human health. This may seem entirely unjustified to us if we think that animal experimentation can only be justified to find better ways to treat human beings.

The scientists point to examples like the biologists studying how some cells in the eye of the fruit fly form as the fly develops. It turns out that the gene that controls the development of these fruit fly cells is also involved in human cancer. Such research has led to the development of a new class of anti-cancer drugs, in a way no one could have predicted at the start.

What about genetically altered animals?

Man has been genetically manipulating other species for thousands of years. Modern sheep and cattle are the result of centuries of selective breeding. Generations of farmers have been aiming to produce animals with suitable wool or with the ability to produce large volumes of milk.

Equally, traditional breeding has generated violent and aggressive breeds of dog such as the pit bull terrier and wolf hybrids.

Transgenic and cloned animals are different because their characteristics have been engineered in a much more precise way than was possible with selective breeding. Arguably there is no moral difference between manipulating animals by breeding or by modern genetics, which is simply a more efficient way of achieving the same ends.

Transgenic animal experiments need to be justified or rejected on the same grounds as other animal experiments. Cloning of animals might be seen as acceptable if it is used to produce new drugs, but the same technology has the potential to be applied to humans, which most people see as abhorrent.

Responding to unjustified animal suffering in experiments

When we have weighed up all the issues we are left with a challenge. Are we concerned enough to act? We might feel that we have to boycott products tested on animals, or protest against some or all of the animal experiments now carried out.

Equally we may want to defend some animal experiments as a means to make people healthier or because we believe that within limits scientists should follow where the scientific story they are investigating leads.

Neither the aggressive arguments of some of the scientific community, nor the bombings committed by animal rights extremists, seem likely to win anyone else over to their sides.

References
1. The Animals (Scientific Procedures) Act 1986.
2. Singer, Peter. *Animal Liberation*. Pimlico. 1975.
3. Genesis 1:26-27.

• The above information is from *CMF files*, a series produced by the Christian Medical Fellowship. It can also be found on their web site. See page 41 for details.
© *Christian Medical Fellowship (CMF)*

Facts and figures on animal research in Great Britain

Information from the Research Defence Society (RDS)

Animal experimentation is a vital part of medical research and safety testing, and is used to study what happens in the whole living body. Animal studies are used alongside other research techniques including study of cells in test tubes, of model systems in computers and of diseases in human populations.

When it is necessary to look at the complex interactions of the body, animals can provide models of human systems. In biomedical and veterinary research and development, where over 90% of laboratory animals are used, there are still many unanswered questions about how the living body works, what goes wrong in disease, and how to develop the best treatments. It is estimated that animal experimentation makes up about 5% of all medical research.

No one wants to use animals unnecessarily or to cause them unnecessary suffering. The guiding principles in animal research today are called the three Rs:

- **Refine** the way experiments are carried out, to make sure animals suffer as little as possible.
- **Reduce** the number of animals used to a minimum.
- **Replace** animal experiments with non-animal techniques wherever possible.

In what areas of research and testing are laboratory animals used?

Animal experimentation is used in several areas of biomedical research and product testing. Using the statistics for 1997 (the last year for which figures are available), it is possible to break down types of animal procedure as follows:

1. Developing new treatments for diseases, or ways of preventing diseases: 43%

2. Fundamental biological and medical research: 31%

3. Safety testing of non-medical products used in the household, agriculture and industry (Less than 0.1% on cosmetics ingredients): 8%

4. Breeding animals with an inherited genetic defect for medical research: 16%

5. Developing new methods of diagnosis: 1%

How much animal research is done?

There were under 3 million scientific procedures using animals in 1997. The exact figure is 2,635,969. The number of animals used is slightly less as some animals are used more than once. This does not happen often, and is strictly controlled.

The annual number of animal experiments has halved over the last 20 years. The number last year was the lowest for 40 years. This fall is due to higher standards of animal welfare, scientific advances and stricter controls. Although there are sometimes small rises, e.g. in 1991, 1994 and 1996, the overall trend is downwards.

The graph below seems to show an increase in 1987. A change in the law in 1986 led to 'procedures', rather than 'experiments', being counted. The definition of procedures is somewhat broader, including the use of animals to produce natural products for research or treatment (about 12% of all procedures).

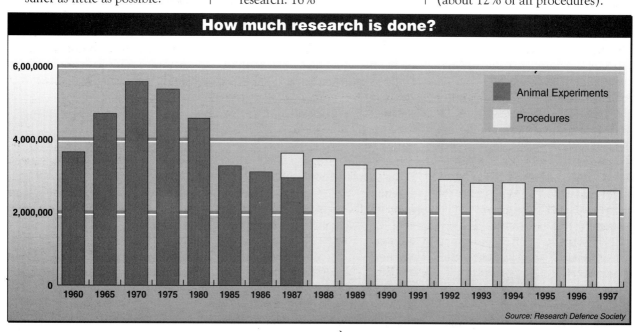

How much research is done?

Source: Research Defence Society

What animals are used in research?

Numbers relate to procedures on animals in Great Britain in 1997.

86% Rats, mice and other rodents. All specially bred laboratory species.

10% Fish, birds, amphibians and reptiles.

1.9% Small mammals other than rodents, mostly rabbits and ferrets.

2.3% Sheep, cows, pigs and other large animals

0.3% Dogs and cats. Specially bred for research. No strays or unwanted pets can be used.

0.2% Monkeys such as marmosets and macaques. The great apes (chimpanzees, orang-utans and gorillas) have not been used in this country for over 18 years.

How is animal research controlled?

There have been special controls on the use of laboratory animals in the UK since 1876. These were revised and extended in 1986 as the Animals (Scientific Procedures) Act. This law safeguards laboratory animal welfare while allowing important medical research to continue. These controls are widely regarded as the strictest in the world.

At the heart of the operation of the Animals (Scientific Procedures) Act 1986 is a cost-benefit analysis which must be applied before any research project involving animals can go ahead. Thus the costs, in terms of potential animal suffering, must be weighed against the potential benefits of the research.

The Act requires that animal procedures:

- take place in research institutes or companies which have appropriate animal accommodation and veterinary facilities, and have gained a certificate of designation
- are part of an approved research or testing programme which has been given a project licence
- are carried out by people with sufficient training, skills and experience as shown in their personal licence.

Licences are only granted if:
- the potential results are important

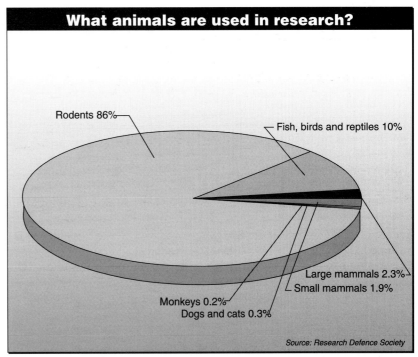

What animals are used in research?

Rodents 86%

Fish, birds and reptiles 10%

Large mammals 2.3%
Small mammals 1.9%

Monkeys 0.2%
Dogs and cats 0.3%

Source: Research Defence Society

enough to justify the use of animals (the cost-benefit analysis)
- the research cannot be done using non-animal methods
- the minimum number of animals will be used
- dogs, cats or primates are only used when other species are not suitable
- any discomfort or suffering is kept to a minimum by appropriate use of anaesthetics or pain killers
- researchers and technicians conducting procedures have the necessary training, skills and experience
- research premises have the necessary facilities to look after the animals properly (laid down in a Home Office Code of Practice).

To ensure that all animal research is done according to these controls, the Home Office employs a team of inspectors, who are all qualified vets or doctors. On average, they visit each research establishment eight times a year. In addition, at each establishment a vet must be on call at all times. Animals must be examined every day and any animal judged to be in severe pain or distress that cannot be relieved must be painlessly killed.

Other relevant regulations

Safety testing is usually carried out so that medicines and other products meet particular UK, foreign or international regulations. In 1997, 20% of scientific procedures were conducted to comply with the provisions of such regulations. Relevant UK laws and regulations include:

- Medicines Act 1986
- Health and Safety at Work Act 1974
- Control of Substances Hazardous to Health 1988
- Control of Pesticides Regulations 1986
- Food and Environment Protection Act 1985
- Food Safety Act 1990
- Consumer Protection Act 1987

New products often have to undergo a range of different tests to meet the requirements of regulatory authorities in different countries. Efforts are now being made to harmonise requirements, which should lead to further reductions in laboratory animal use.

Information sources:
Statistics of Scientific Procedures on Living Animals, Great Britain 1997, HMSO.
Guidance on the Operation of the Animals (Scientific Procedures) Act 1986, HMSO.
The Use of Animals in Research, Development and Testing, 1992, Parliamentary Office of Science and Technology.

Cosmetics and product testing

Information from Animal Aid

Every year tens of thousands of animals die having suffered misery and pain in experiments carried out to develop cosmetics, toiletries and household products such as soaps, shampoos, deodorants, washing powders, bleaches, glues, paints, weed killers, and even food additives such as colourings and preservatives. Animals are also used in experiments to test agricultural chemicals such as pesticides and herbicides, and industrial chemicals such as solvents and lubricants.

Why are cosmetics and other products tested on animals?

The law doesn't say that cosmetics and other products have to be tested on animals, only that companies must ensure that their products are safe for people to use and that they will not damage the environment. European guidelines, however, recommend that companies perform animal experiments before they market new ingredients, so animal tests are still used by most manufacturers. Presently in the UK, there is a 'voluntary ban' on the testing of finished cosmetic products on animals. However most animal testing takes place during the development of new ingredients and this will not be affected by the ban.

What sorts of tests are performed?

Toxicity test

In these poisoning tests a particular substance is added to the food or water, or is force fed to them through a long syringe directly into the stomach. After they have been dosed with the substance, the animals are watched for any symptoms of poisoning, such as tremors, bleeding, vomiting or loss of balance. The test may last for many days and any animals that do not die of poisoning during the experiment are killed and autopsied (examined). These tests are usually conducted on rats and mice.

Skin irritancy test

This test involves shaving and scratching a patch of a guinea pig or rabbit's skin before applying the test substance. The animals are often held in a restraining device to stop them licking or rubbing the test area. Again, they are observed for any symptoms of poisoning or sensitivity, such as reddening, swelling, cracking, bleeding or ulceration of the skin. The test lasts for several days and no pain relief is given.

Eye irritancy test

During the Draize test a substance is dripped into the eyes of rabbits to see if it causes any irritation or damage. During the test, which lasts for several days, the unfortunate animals are held in stocks to stop them wiping or rubbing their eyes. They are given no pain relief. Rabbits are used because they have large eyes and because they have poor tear ducts which means they can't wash away the test substance. This test procedure, like all the others, can cause great pain and suffering.

The nonsense of it all is that these cruel tests don't make products any safer. Many experts now say that such animal experiments are crude and unscientific. Animals often react to substances differently to humans, so animal tests give results that don't necessarily apply to humans. In poisoning tests animals are often given much larger doses of a substance than humans would ever use.

How else can we test for safety?

The best option would be not to do the tests. There are already thousands of ingredients for cosmetics and household products – do we really need any more? The companies that produce 'cruelty-free' products use mild and natural ingredients that are known to be safe because they have been used by people for many years.

As long as companies continue to produce new ingredients for cosmetics and other products there will be a need to test them for safety. The long-term answer, then, is to replace animal tests with humane alternative ones. In fact, there already exist various computer models and tests involving the use of human tissue or cell cultures, which could replace all the standard safety procedures. Because they are based on human data, they also have the added benefit that they provide much more reliable results.

Guide to cruelty-free shopping

The best way to encourage manufacturers to change their policy on animal testing is to use your consumer power and only buy 'cruelty-free' non-animal tested products.

The trouble is, buying 'cruelty free' isn't as straightforward as it first appears. The various 'cruelty-free' or 'animal-friendly' claims made by the different companies can be pretty confusing because there is no standard way of labelling products.

Another problem is that nearly all the ingredients for cosmetics and household products will have been tested on animals at some time in the past.

The main cruelty-free policies are:

Fixed cut-off date

This means the products do not contain any ingredients that have been tested on animals after a certain date. Some ingredients may have been tested before this 'cut-off date' (and as already stated, most ingredients will have been tested at some point in the past), but the company is not supporting animal testing that has taken place since. Most importantly, the company is not encouraging more animal tests to take place as it will only use ingredients already in existence. The 'cut-off date' varies between companies, but the best one to look for is 1978.

Five-year rule

This means the product contains ingredients which have not been tested on animals during the previous five years. However, ingredients that were tested on animals, say, six years before could be included. It can take around five years for a newly tested ingredient to become available for use in products anyway, so this policy on its own will not encourage an end to animal tests. After all, an ingredient being tested today could be used by the manufacturer in five years' time.

Companies

Here are some companies which have a fixed cut-off date policy. Their ranges are mostly available from health food shops, but you may find some in supermarkets and other shops. Most of the companies have a mail order service too, so write to us enclosing a SAE if you would like the address of any companies listed.

'Vg' indicates that none of the products contain any animal ingredients and are suitable for vegans. 'Vt' indicates that some of the products may contain animal ingredients, but will be suitable for vegetarians. NV indicates that some products may contain non-vegetarian ingredients such as gelatine.

Household products:

Bio-D	Vg
Caurnie Soap Co.	Vg
Clear Spring	Vg
Co-op (own brand)	NV
Home Care Products	Vg
Honesty	Vg
Janco Sales	Vg
Little Green Shop	

Cosmetics:

Animal Aid	Vg
Beauty without Cruelty	Vt

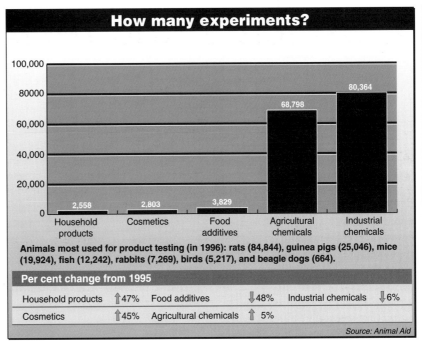

How many experiments?

Household products: 2,558
Cosmetics: 2,803
Food additives: 3,829
Agricultural chemicals: 68,798
Industrial chemicals: 80,364

Animals most used for product testing (in 1996): rats (84,844), guinea pigs (25,046), mice (19,924), fish (12,242), rabbits (7,269), birds (5,217), and beagle dogs (664).

Per cent change from 1995					
Household products	↑47%	Food additives	↓48%	Industrial chemicals	↓6%
Cosmetics	↑45%	Agricultural chemicals	↑5%		

Source: Animal Aid

Bodyline	Vg
Body Shop (cosmetics)	NV
Caurnie Soap Co.	Vg
Cosmetics to Go	Vt
Co-op (own brand)	NV
Creighton's Naturally	Vt
Daniel Field	Vg
Faith in Nature	Vg
Honesty Cosmetics	Vg
Montagne Jeunesse	Vt
Pure Plant Products	Vg
Weleda	Vt

Beware of animal ingredients

Watch out for animal ingredients in cosmetics, toiletries and household products.

Soaps and creams are sometimes made with animal fats such as tallow and lard.

Shampoos can contain animal protein and some cosmetics contain gelatine, animal glycerine, collagen and placental cells which are all slaughterhouse products. Bath pearls usually contain gelatine.

Expensive perfumes sometimes contain real musk (scraped from musk pods of the male musk deer), civet and castoreum (which are extracted from the anal sex glands of civet cats and beavers respectively).

Beware if labels say:

'Product not tested on animals'
The ingredients may have been tested on animals. In fact, most animal testing is for ingredients and not finished products.

'We (the company) do not perform tests on animals'
The product and ingredients may have been tested on animals by someone else.

'Contains only natural ingredients'
'Natural' or not, they may have been tested on animals.

'Environmentally friendly product'
This doesn't always mean 'animal friendly'. 'Green' or 'environmentally friendly' may have been tested on animals.

In brief

The golden rule is check the label!

Remember, most of the big companies and supermarkets that product cosmetics and household products still use animal experiments and ingredients.

Unless a product has a label saying that it has not been tested on animals then you can assume it has.

On labels you should look for two things:
1. That neither the product or its ingredients have been tested on animals
2. That the product contains no animal ingredients

If in doubt, write to the manufacturer for clarification of their animal testing policy.

• The above information is from Animal Aid. See page 41 for address details.

© Animal Aid

The responsible way forward in bodycare

Animal testing: your questions answered . . .

Our industry is committed to the ultimate elimination of animal testing and shares public concern about the use of animals in the safety assessment of cosmetic and toiletry products.

We are also committed to the highest possible standards of consumer and employee safety. As all cosmetics and toiletries are applied directly to the human body, it is essential to ensure that they are safe to use.

The majority of our products are made from ingredients which have a known safety record, and do not require animal testing.

This information aims to explain the CTPA's position on animal testing, to dispel some of the misunderstandings about the issue and to answer the most common questions we are asked. We have looked at three key areas:
1. The background
2. Safety assessment
3. The search for alternatives

1. The background

Q. 'What is meant by cosmetics?'
A. To most consumers the word cosmetics means lipsticks, mascaras, eyeshadows and face powder, but the legal definition is quite different and covers a much wider range of products. The majority of our industry's products are items such as toothpaste, soap, deodorants, sunscreens, skin and hair care preparations; products used every day by practically everyone. All of these are applied directly to the external surface of the body, e.g. the skin or mouth. It is therefore essential that they are safe.

Q. 'What is safety testing?'
A. Safety testing involves a range of assessments which can include animal testing where no alternative can provide comparable results.

Within our industry, the safety of a finished product can generally be assessed from a knowledge of the ingredients: consequently most finished products are not tested on animals.

Q. 'Are animals used for testing cosmetic products?'
A. Animals are no longer used for safety testing of finished products, their safety is generally assessed from a knowledge of the ingredients. In 1996 only 252 were used in the UK for this purpose, and in November 1997 the commercial contract laboratories undertaking the work voluntarily gave up their Home Office licences.

Q. 'What is meant by "cruelty free" and "not tested on animals"?'
A. The terms 'cruelty free' and 'not tested on animals' are difficult to define as they are subject to a wide number of interpretations by different companies, organisations and regulatory bodies. Factors taken into account can include the origin of the ingredients and the time since the last known tests took place. Some companies base their 'cruelty free' or 'not tested on animals' statements on the fact that neither they, nor their suppliers, have carried out or commissioned animal tests on finished products. Other companies base claims on a time frame of five or ten years, either on a fixed or rolling basis in relation to both the products and ingredients. There are also

manufacturers who will not use ingredients which have been introduced since 1976 or 1978, these being the dates of introduction and implementation of the 1976 EC Directive. Customers should refer to individual company policy statements for details.

Q. 'Is the LD50 test used nowadays?'
A. The LD50 test is no longer used by the cosmetics and toiletries industry.

In 1984 the CTPA Council issued a statement urging its member companies to press their suppliers of ingredients to carry out 'limit' tests rather than LD50 tests, to establish safety.

Q. 'Is any acute oral toxicity testing necessary?'
A. Most cosmetics are, by nature, unlikely to be harmful when swallowed, and manufacturers normally do not carry out acute oral testing. Information on a product's oral toxicity is essential for poison centres to determine if a product swallowed by a child will be harmful. In most cases this will be predicted by a knowledge of the toxicity of the ingredient contained in databases. When some estimate of acute toxicity is necessary to provide assurance of consumer safety, companies generally use alternative procedures such as internationally agreed 'limit' tests which are reduction and refinement tests, rather than true animal replacements. The dose administered is restricted to the amount likely to be ingested by man and the minimum number of animals is used. If, as is normally the case with cosmetics, there are no serious adverse effects, no further testing is required. Since death is not an end point, the animals can be humanely killed at the first sign of distress and therefore suffering is considerably reduced.

Q. 'What about the Draize eye test?'
A. There is a great deal of false information in circulation concerning eye irritancy testing. The classic Draize eye test, where an ingredient is placed into one of the eyes of several animals (usually rabbits) and the effects observed over a period of 1 to 72 hours, is not used for cosmetic and toiletry testing.

Q. 'Is any eye testing necessary?'
A. The eye is a very important and vulnerable organ and, because many products are applied to the eye area, manufacturers must exercise great care to ensure that no damage can arise.

Since many of our ingredients are used in other industries, the eye irritation potential is often known, and the irritancy of a cosmetic product can therefore be predicted without recourse to experiments. If a novel ingredient is used, very strong irritants can readily be assessed by in-vitro (non-animal) methods. Where confirmation of low or nil irritancy response is required, test procedures involving the dilution of substances can be used so that a mild response is produced. A single animal is used in the initial test.

Alternative laboratory procedures not using animals have been introduced by a number of CTPA member companies and are used as preliminary screening procedures. Unfortunately, despite several major international validation studies, no one test has been accepted by Government regulators.

2. Safety assessment
Q. 'How is the safety of ingredients assessed?'
A. Most of our ingredients have been widely used for many years and there is a wealth of toxicological safety information from the scientific literature, databases and in use experience. In the vast majority of cases safety can be assessed from this knowledge. Where confirmatory tests are necessary, human volunteers are used to the maximum extent possible, and only rarely is it necessary to use animals.

Q. 'Why test on animals at all?'
A. The need for animal testing arises primarily with the introduction of new ingredients. Only when all available and validated non-animal alternatives have been used and some human safety concern remains is animal testing considered. The benefits of new ingredients include:
- Human health, for example, anti-plaque/tartar agents, UV filters
- Human safety, for example, preservative systems
- Environmental improvement such as biodegradability.

Some companies have a policy whereby they will not use any new ingredient which has involved animal testing. As European Community legislation requires animal testing in some circumstances this limits the range of products which these companies can introduce, particularly in relation to active or new ingredients or existing ingredients whose safety has been challenged.

Q. 'What does the industry look for?'
A. When assessing the safety of either a completely new or reformulated product, there are a number of different aspects that must be considered. In 99% of cases, manufacturers already know the answers.

These factors are:
Skin irritation
Companies need to know whether their product will cause irritation when in contact with human skin.
Eye irritation
Information on eye irritancy is normally available from suppliers, and can sometimes also be judged from skin irritation information.
Oral toxicity
Information on oral toxicity is needed to establish, for example, whether a product could be harmful if swallowed accidentally by a child. This can usually be assessed from raw material data. Results gained from oral toxicity tests are supplied to the National Poisons Unit, for use by hospitals in accidents or emergencies.

3. The search for alternatives
Q. 'How many tests involve the use of animals?'
A. In 1997, the last year for which figures are available, the total number of scientific procedures involving animals was approximately 2.64 million of which 1,300 animals were used for the safety evaluation of cosmetics and toiletries.

Q. 'What are the alternative tests?'
The industry continues to develop alternative procedures to replace the

need for animal tests. These alternatives are used whenever possible in all fields of research including routine safety clearance and pre-screening. These tests include:

- Making optimal use of existing information, through improved storage and exchange of available data, so that the necessary duplication of tests on animals can be avoided.
- Use of computer modelling relating the structural and biological properties of molecules (quantitative structural/activity relationships – QSAR).
- Use of computer graphics and molecular modelling to design in desirable characteristics and design out the potential for adverse effects.
- Computer modelling and simulation of physiological and toxicological processes, to predict the potential fate and effects of substances that enter the body.
- Test involving physico-chemical methods not involving living organisms as in the EYTEX test as a replacement for the Draize eye irritancy test.
- Use of 'in-vitro' methods, including the short-term maintenance of whole organs, tissue slices,

cell suspensions or cell fractions, and long-term cell and organ culture. For example, specific methods such as the dye release method developed by FRAME or the use of bovine corneas, can contribute to a battery of methods for replacing the Draize eye irritancy test.

- Tests involving lower organisms, i.e. invertebrates, plants and microorganisms, as in genotoxicity tests on bacteria.
- Human studies – including the strictly-controlled use of human volunteers, and epidemiological and post-marketing surveys.

To achieve the industry's stated goal of eliminating the need for animal testing it is essential that the regulatory authorities accept the use of such alternatives.

Q. 'What progress is being made on alternatives?'

A. Before a non-animal test can be accepted as a full replacement for an animal test it must be shown that when it is carried out by different individuals in different laboratories it gives consistently 'valid' results. Much of the work and expense involved in the development of alternatives is devoted to validation.

Q. 'What is the way forward?'

A. Our industry is committed to the ultimate elimination of animal testing. However, realistically this will not be achieved in the immediate future. In the meantime progress is being made by the consistent application of the '3R's' policy:

- To reduce the need for animal testing to an absolute minimum
- To refine the tests to make them more acceptable, both by refinement of methods and reduction in the number of animals involved per test
- To replace the tests using live animals by alternative methods thus eliminating all animal testing. This can be done through better management of information and the development of alternative testing.

Q. 'What will the future bring?'

A. The Cosmetic Directive has been amended so that animal testing will not be permitted after 30 June 2000 if validated non-animal alternative methods are available. This will in effect make it mandatory to use alternatives where these are accepted by the regulatory authorities.

A necessary evil?

Animal experimenters claim that their research is vital to find cures for diseases. They say it is a choice between your dog or your child. But is it?

A lesson from history

It seems that whenever a campaign to end cruel and unjust practices becomes popular, those who want things to stay as they are argue that any change will cause huge problems. They also describe campaigners for change as 'dangerous extremists'. When the campaign to abolish slavery gained support, those people who wanted the slave system to continue argued that society and industry would practically collapse without it. Their grim warnings came to nothing.

Children in this country were once forced to work in mines, factories and as chimney sweeps.

Women were denied the right to vote in elections. These practices were similarly defended.

The problem with animal experiments

Apart from the suffering they cause, animal experiments produce results that are unreliable.

That's because animals don't get the same illnesses as we do and because their bodies work differently from ours. Animals develop different sorts of cancer and heart disease, whilst the use of monkeys in polio research delayed a proper understanding of the disease by more than 25 years.

Animals also react to drugs differently from us. For example, useful drugs like aspirin and paracetamol are highly poisonous to cats, while penicillin kills guinea pigs and hamsters. Many drugs which were passed 'safe' in animal tests have had to be withdrawn after causing dangerous side-effects when given to people. Even scientists admit that it is only when trials have taken place in humans that we can tell whether or not a new drug is safe, or if a new surgical technique really will save lives. Animal experiments are a very hit-and-miss method and should not be trusted. By giving misleading information, they have actually delayed progress, too. For example, the link between smoking and lung cancer was first observed in people, but because scientists could not 'prove' it with animal experiments (no animal developed lung cancer when made to breathe tobacco smoke), vital health warnings were delayed for many years.

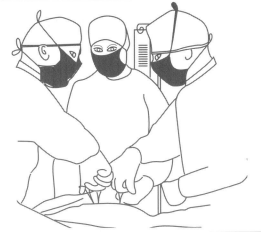

How disease is defeated

The single most important aspect of health care is the prevention of disease. In the last century, infectious diseases such as tuberculosis, typhoid, smallpox and whooping cough killed people in huge numbers. These diseases were not defeated by medicine – death rates were already falling fast before medical treatment became available – but by social improvements such as better food, living and working conditions, clean water and proper working toilets and drains.

The poverty trap

In poorer countries, the main causes of death today are the poverty-linked diseases that killed so many in the UK a hundred years ago. According to the poverty-relief charity Oxfam, 25,000 children die every year from diseases associated with dirty water, 2 billion people have no access to clean water and 3 billion have no sanitation.

Even in this country, social conditions remain the most important factor in health. Poorer people are more likely to suffer from heart disease, cancer and many other illnesses. In his book, *The Trouble With Medicine*, Dr Melvin Konner explains how 'poverty today brings with it lack of access to medical care, as well as abuse of cigarettes, alcohol, street drugs and food, not to mention prostitution and violence – all major

routes to current deaths amongst the poor . . . The social conditions that helped cause the nineteenth-century scourges are at least equally implicated in our own twentieth-century ones.'[1]

Even though medicine is limited in the influence it can have on health, it has, of course, saved many lives and it is vital that the search for improved treatments continues. This does not mean that animal experiments must continue.

Humane research

It is easy to show that stopping animal experiments would not mean an end to medical progress. Just look at the times when researchers could not use animals and had to invent another method. For example, vaccines are mostly tested on animals, but because animals don't usually develop pneumonia, scientists had to find another way to test the pneumonia vaccine. They did so by chemical analysis and studies with human volunteers.

A limited amount of useful information may have come – purely by chance – from animal experiments, but other methods offer hope for real progress. Concentrating on human data will provide reliable evidence for building an effective health policy.

Anti-vivisectionists want to see cures for diseases as much as everybody else, but recognise that medical scientists can't work miracles and that hurting animals in laboratories won't improve human health. The most important factors in the search for improved health are still disease prevention and the fight against poverty.

Above all, people who oppose animal experiments believe that it is cruel and unjust to inflict pain and misery on animals in laboratories.

Research without animals

With all the pro-vivisection propaganda, it is easy to forget that using animals is only one of many methods of research. Others include:

Epidemiology – groups of people are studied and compared to discover the causes of disease. The links between lung cancer and smoking and between heart disease and a fatty diet were both found by this method.

Clinical case studies – careful observation and monitoring of diseases in individual patients, plus the use of high-tech devices such as body scanners.

Post-mortem studies – doctors can discover clues about disease by close examination of the bodies of people who have died.

Studies with healthy volunteers – to investigate how the human body functions.

Test-tube experiments – human cells can be used to develop and test drugs and for the manufacture of products like vaccines and antibodies.

Computer technology – imitating the human body and its workings for medical research and in teaching.

Pause for thought

Do you think it is right to use animals in experiments related to
- cosmetics?
- household products?
- military weapons?
- medical products?

References
1. Dr Melvin Konner, *The Trouble with Medicine*, BBC Books, 1993.

• The above is an extract from *Why Animal Rights?*, produced by Animal Aid. See page 41 for address details.
© *Animal Aid*

Animal research

Animal research and the development of new medicines

Summary

Turning a scientific theory into a new medicine now takes, on average, 12 years. During that time, computer models of new molecules will be studied, thousands of variations will be investigated in the test-tube and a small number will go on to be studied in animals. Then, if doctors and scientists are confident they can do so without undue risks, the potential new medicine will be studied in people.

Animal research is essential to help scientists evaluate the safety and effectiveness of new medicines. This is because most of those effects of a new medicine which are not yet predictable by using computer models or test-tube research can be seen in well-designed and conducted animal studies.

The biological similarities between ourselves and other animals are enormous. Animal research therefore provides essential guidance enabling researchers to bridge the gap between the test-tube and the patient. There are, of course, species differences between ourselves and other animals but compared to the similarities, the differences are minor and can usually be taken into account.

Animal research is not a cheap option and is conducted under strict UK legislative controls.

Unexpected effects

Even after years of intensive study, and a comprehensive evaluation of all the data by both the originating company and the Government's licensing authority, medicines sometimes cause unexpected side-effects in general use. Those who campaign against animal research frequently cite such side-effects as an argument against animal testing but this is to misunderstand the careful step-by-step nature of the research process.

No one expects animal studies to provide all the necessary information and final decisions are never made on the basis of animal tests alone. Rather, they enable researchers to move as close as possible to the human situation, before a new medicine is tested and used in people. All medicines approved since the introduction of the Medicines Act 1968, including ones later found to have unexpected effects, passed all the testing stages including non-animal, animal and human research.

No amount of testing can guarantee to find all possible side-effects for every person who may take a medicine. A reaction which occurs at a rate of one in 100,000 people or even at a higher rate of one in 10,000, for instance, may not be seen until very large numbers of people use the medicine.

Do computers help?

Computers have made research much more efficient and have therefore helped to reduce the number of animals needed. Computers have been particularly important in the design of potential new medicines, where existing knowledge is used to 'design in' features that could be helpful and 'design out' features likely to cause harm.

But however advanced technology has become, biological knowledge is still limited and computer modelling only makes theoretical molecules. This is a long way from testing a real medicine in the living body. As knowledge of our biology increases, so too will the contribution computers make to medicines research.

Can cell culture be used more?

Cell culture work in the test-tube is used wherever possible and its usefulness will continue to increase as knowledge improves of how our cells work in the body. This is desirable not only for humane reasons but also because today's cell culture work is much cheaper and faster than the animal tests it replaced.

Cell cultures do not, however, tell us about the range of effects (both helpful and harmful) which only occur when a medicine is in the complete living body, as opposed to cells in isolation.

How is animal research regulated?

The Animals (Scientific Procedures) Act 1986 aims to strike a balance between the needs of research and the welfare of laboratory animals.

The main requirements of the Animals (Scientific Procedures) Act 1986 are that:

- Only competent people can conduct the research;
- Research premises must have the staff and facilities to look after the animals properly before, during and after procedures;
- The likely benefits of the research must justify any possible distress to the animals.

The law also aims to ensure that studies are well designed so that as few animals as possible are needed and requires that non-animal alternatives are used wherever applicable. Where animals are needed, appropriate steps must be taken to ensure that any distress they may experience is kept to the minimum possible given the nature of the research. Proper veterinary care must be provided at all times.

Most laboratory animals experience little or only momentary pain but where more pain is likely, researchers must plan in advance how they will prevent or relieve it. If an animal is in severe distress which cannot be alleviated it must, by law, be humanely killed immediately regardless of whether the purpose of the research has been achieved.

Home Office approval of each research project must be granted before the work can begin and their inspectors regularly visit laboratories, often unannounced, to check that the Act's requirements are being followed.

Will the number of animals needed be reduced?

Researchers aim to use the smallest number of animals necessary in the development of new and improved medical treatments. Advances in biological knowledge and new technology have led to big reductions in the number of animals needed in many areas. Over the past 20 years, the total has fallen by nearly half.

However, this does not mean that there will automatically be reductions year after year in the number of procedures involving animals across the research spectrum. Some years show small increases because of new areas of research.

For example, with the help of transgenic animals, researchers are now able to study the genetic basis of illness in a way that has not been possible in the past. This work is bringing real hope for people living with many hitherto untreatable, or inadequately treated, conditions. In addition, new public health concerns, such as BSE, will arise from time to time and need to be investigated.

Furthermore, UK pharmaceutical companies that successfully develop new medicines may be able to increase their research programmes. This may make overall reductions more difficult to achieve. The pharmaceutical industry wants to reduce the use of animals in research but only insofar as this can be done without compromising human health.

Is the pharmaceutical industry committed to animal welfare?

The UK pharmaceutical industry fully recognises its responsibility to obey the spirit as well as the letter of the law. The ABPI believes that all organisations under whose auspices research is conducted must ensure that they create a culture which embodies the principles and encourages the day-to-day practice of good animal welfare. The UK pharmaceutical industry has a well-deserved reputation for high standards of laboratory animal welfare.

The ABPI is also taking a major role in international discussions between the pharmaceutical industry of the US, the EU and Japan, along with their respective medicines regulatory authorities, to ensure that those tests demanded by Governments around the world are consistent so that duplication or unnecessary animal research is eliminated.

© *The Association of the British Pharmaceutical Industry (ABPI)*

Primates in research & testing

Every year over 3,500 primates are used in UK laboratories. The RSPCA is extremely concerned about the suffering caused to these highly intelligent animals

What is a primate?

Monkeys, apes and humans are all part of the same group of animals called primates. Primates are all descended from a shared ancestor. Apes, such as chimpanzees and gorillas, are the most closely related primates to humans. Monkeys are the biggest group with over 120 species, ranging in size from the largest baboon to the tiny pygmy marmoset. Monkeys are divided into two main groups depending on where they come from. Old World monkeys come from Africa and Asia and include macaques, baboons, and langurs. New World monkeys come from South America and include spider monkeys, squirrel monkeys, capuchins, marmosets and tamarins.

The term non-human primate is often used to differentiate between humans and other primates.

Special concern

Non-human primates are very intelligent animals. They are closely related to humans with highly developed brains, complicated patterns of behaviour and intricate social relationships. Furthermore, they are likely to have an awareness of pain, suffering and distress that is similar in nature to that of humans. These factors make their use in scientific research a matter of particular ethical concern.

In addition, there can be serious distress involved in the acquisition and importation of primates and the conditions under which they are kept in laboratories are seldom adequate to meet their complex needs. The RSPCA therefore has special concern over the use of non-human primates in any research and testing.

Human substitutes

Non-human primates have very similar body systems and patterns of behaviour to humans because they are so closely related to us. For this reason they are used in research as substitutes for humans. Scientists claim they can find out more relevant information from non-human primates than from other animals because of this close biological similarity.

Chimpanzees

Chimpanzees are our closest primate relatives, sharing over 97 per cent of our genetic make-up. No chimpanzees or other apes have been used in the UK since the introduction of the Animals (Scientific Procedures) Act 1986, which controls the use of living animals in experiments, but they are still used in other countries, such as the USA and the Netherlands.

Areas of research

Most scientific procedures that involve primates are carried out to develop or test new medical products or procedures. These include the development of new drugs to treat conditions such as Alzheimer's and Parkinson's diseases, or new techniques such as transplant surgery. In 1994, 83 per cent of the 5,163 procedures carried out on primates were associated with medical research. The remaining 17 per cent of procedures were conducted for other reasons, for example, for basic biological research.

Marmosets

Common marmosets (*Callithrix jacchus*) are the smallest primates used in UK research. They weigh about 350g and can live for up to 17 years in captivity. Marmosets are arboreal (tree-living) monkeys which live in family groups consisting of a breeding pair and up to three sets of twin offspring. They originate from the South American rain forest, but most of those used in the UK are purpose-bred in Britain.

Macaques

Macaques are the most widely distributed non-human primate group, and are found all over Asia and North Africa. Two species are commonly used in research: the long-tailed or crab-eating macaque (*Macaca fascicularis*) and the rhesus macaque (*Macaca mulatta*). Macaques are medium-sized, weighing 4-10kg, and can live for up to 30 years. In the wild, macaques live in mixed-sex groups with several females to each male. The complicated social relationships within each group are maintained by elaborate communication systems. Although some macaques are bred in the UK, most of those used are imported from captive breeding centres outside Europe such as in the Philippines and Mauritius.

Other primates

Baboons, squirrel monkeys, cotton-top tamarins and occasionally other monkeys are also used in research. The choice of species used will depend on a number of factors, including the type of research conducted, the suitability of the species for the study, availability of animals, and existing background information on the species.

International trade

Around half of the monkeys in UK laboratories are imported from outside Europe. This international trade in primates is one of the most disturbing aspects of their use. The UK imports more primates than any other country in the European Union – around 2,500 each year. Almost all of these are destined for use in research or testing.

Until recently most of the primates used in UK research were taken from the wild. In 1995, the RSPCA made a series of recommendations to the Government which resulted in a ban on the use of wild-caught primates except in cases of 'exceptional and specific justification'. Over 97 per cent of imported primates now come from captive-bred sources. Baboons are the only wild-caught primates still being used in the UK.

Controls on the import and use of primates

Trade in primates is covered by the Convention on International Trade in Endangered Species (CITES). This means that a permit is needed to move any primate from one country to another. Primates transported by air must travel in accordance with the International Air Transport Association (IATA) regulations. But controls on primate housing and care outside the UK vary considerably, with many countries having no formal regulations.

Once they arrive in Britain, the use of primates in research and testing is regulated by the Animals (Scientific Procedures) Act 1986. Under this Act, researchers are required to provide special justification for using primates rather than other species for their work.

Working for primates

Scientific procedures carried out on primates cause pain, suffering or distress. This is compounded by the stress of long-distance transportation and the inadequacy of laboratory housing for these remarkable animals.

The RSPCA works to help laboratory primates by seriously questioning why they are used, how they are acquired, and how they are cared for. The Society believes that the necessity and justification for all primate use should be critically reviewed at a national and international level.

The RSPCA is committed to ending the suffering of laboratory primates and calls for:

- A complete ban on the use of wild-caught primates.
- Critical review of all research and testing involving primates.
- Major improvements in conditions for all laboratory primates consistent with their behavioural, social and physical needs.

If you are concerned about the use of primates in laboratories you can help by making your views known to the UK Government. Write to your MP or the Home Secretary (Home Office, 50 Queen Anne's Gate, London SW1H 9AT) with your concerns.

© RSPCA

Animal welfare in the laboratory

Information from the Research Defence Society (RDS)

There are two basic questions which should be asked about using animals in experiments: 'Is it necessary?' and 'Is it cruel?' Most of this information is aimed at answering the first of these questions by demonstrating that most important medical advances have depended on animal research and that there are still a large number of areas in modern medical science which require studies on laboratory animals. However, the welfare of laboratory animals is an essential part of animal research. Medical researchers in the United Kingdom work within a very strict framework of regulations, codes of practice, policies and laws designed to safeguard the welfare of animals used in biomedical research and testing.

The basic principles of laboratory animal welfare were defined in 1959 by William Russell and Rex Burch who proposed the three Rs – Reduce, Refine and Replace. These were proposed as the objectives we should always strive for in animal experimentation: reducing the numbers of animals used to the minimum necessary for the experiment, refining the design of the experiment so as to reduce any harmful effect on the animals as far as possible and replacing animal experiments with non-animal experimental techniques whenever possible. These principles are now accepted in the UK and in many other countries as the fundamental rules of laboratory animal welfare.

Reduce

There are many ways in which one can reduce the numbers of animals used in an experiment. It is very important to carry out a proper statistical analysis of the proposed experiment to determine how many animals need to be used. If too few animals are used then the results of

the experiment are not reliable and it needs to be repeated, using more animals. Use too many animals and the results are still reliable, but animal life has been wasted. To reduce the number of animals used to the minimum, the correct number of animals must be used the first time.

It is also important that all other aspects of the experiment are properly designed and carried out correctly. If the experiment fails and needs to be repeated, animals will have been used unnecessarily.

Another way of reducing the number of animals used in an experiment is to use genetically identical animals. This prevents variation in the results from genetic variations between individual animals and thus makes it possible to get reliable answers using fewer animals.

A reduction in the numbers of animals used can also be achieved if the animals are born and bred in ultra-clean conditions and are free of any infections or illnesses which might otherwise interfere with the experimental results.

Refine

Research involving animals has to be designed so that any distress or suffering involved is kept to a minimum. For example, if the experiment would hurt the animal, an anaesthetic or painkiller would normally be given.

If an experiment involves taking repeated blood samples from an animal to measure, for example, the level of a particular hormone, it may be possible to implant a small device to continuously monitor the hormone. This can be done with a simple operation under anaesthetic, so that the animal does not have to be repeatedly caught, restrained and blood taken by syringe.

If an experiment involves animals with a painful or fatal disease, it can be designed so that the animals are painlessly killed at an early stage of the disease, when they only show mild symptoms, instead of waiting until they are clearly dying.

In some cases it is possible to develop a whole new way of conducting a test involving fewer animals. The LD50 test has been used for many years to find out how poisonous chemicals are. The way the test is designed means that some of the animals have to be given a fatal dose of a poisonous chemical. However, scientists have now developed a new test, called the Fixed Dose Procedure, to do the same job. This technique uses fewer animals and is designed so that none of them receive a fatal dose of the poison.

Laboratory animals spend most of their lives simply living in the animal house and not being used in an experiment, so it is important to consider their living conditions. In the past, laboratory animals would often be kept alone in barren cages. These days we prefer to keep animals in social groups, preferably in large cages or floor pens, with things for them to use. Rabbits would be given bedding material, boxes and tubes. Rodents like to have nesting material. Dogs like running in groups and having human company. Monkeys like branches to climb, swings, ropes and platforms. Their diet can also be made much more interesting with fruit and other titbits. Some of these can be mixed in with wood shavings so that they have to forage for their food – a favourite activity.

Replace

A lot of scientific effort has been devoted to developing new, non-animal techniques which can be used in experiments instead of animals. There have been some notable successes, but overall, progress has been disappointingly slow.

The LAL test can now be used to test for pyrogens. Bacteria often shed little bits of their outer covering. If these substances, known as pyrogens, get into the bloodstream, they raise the body temperature. Even very tiny levels of pyrogens cause a dangerous temperature rise, so any liquid going to be injected or fed into a patient's blood stream has to be tested for pyrogen contamination. Previously this was done by injecting the liquid into a rabbit and monitoring the animal's body temperature. The new LAL test uses white blood cells taken from the horseshoe crab which can detect the pyrogens in a test-tube.

Insulin is a lifeline for millions of diabetics, but it is essential they give themselves the correct dose – either too high or too low a dose can be harmful. Each batch of insulin has to be tested to measure how active it is so that the correct dosage can be calculated. Previously, this was done by injecting the insulin into mice, but a new technique has been developed which uses a machine called a chromatograph which can provide the same information, replacing the need to use animals.

Many non-animal techniques have been designed to replace the animal tests used in safety testing, but these new techniques do not always work well enough. A great amount of scientific work has been devoted to the search for a non-animal test to replace the Draize eye irritation test. This test studies whether a chemical irritates the eye by dropping a dilution of it directly onto the eye of an animal, usually a rabbit. Several different non-animal tests have been designed and have all been assessed to see if they accurately predict whether a substance will irritate the eye. Unfortunately, none of them worked well enough to be used to replace the existing animal test. Work is continuing to find a replacement for the Draize test.

Looking after laboratory animals

Laboratory animals are looked after by specially trained animal technicians, who are responsible for ensuring that animals are properly housed, fed and cared for. Every place using laboratory animals has to have a veterinary surgeon constantly on call in case of any welfare problems. Many of these places employ full-time laboratory animal vets.

The buildings where laboratory animals are housed and where the experiments are performed have to be specially designed to meet strict guidelines covering the living conditions of the animals, including minimum amounts of space per animal, room temperature, lighting, ventilation and humidity levels. It is estimated that, in the UK alone, £800 million has been spent in the last 10 years on new buildings and facilities to house laboratory animals. Whilst this may seem a huge amount of money, it serves to demonstrate the value placed upon the welfare of laboratory animals.

• The above is an extract from *Animal research and medical advances*, produced by the Research Defence Society (RDS). See page 41 for address details.

© Research Defence Society (RDS)

Animal rights

Why should it concern me? Information from People for the Ethical Treatment of Animals (PETA)

'Aren't humans more important than animals?'

In fact, humans are animals, though we call the others 'animals' in order to separate ourselves from them so that we will feel less uncomfortable exploiting them. Much as slave owners convinced themselves that black people did not have the same physical and emotional feelings as white people, we have reduced other-than-human beings to virtual automatons, incapable of thinking or experiencing pain, love, joy, sadness or other emotions.

René Descartes, an 18th-century philosopher, believed that the sounds dogs made when he cut into them were no different from or more important than the noises made by machines. He did not recognise dogs as sentient beings. Until very recently, it was common for physicians to perform major surgery without anaesthesia on newborn and premature infants, but paediatricians and others now question this practice. Similarly, many animal experimenters have abandoned this old-fashioned perspective to speak out against vivisection.

'Aren't animals here for us to use?'

Like us, the other animals are valuable in and of themselves, not merely as commodities to be hunted or killed for casseroles and coats or used as living toys and test tubes. Each animal is an individual whose life is as dear to him or her as ours is to us. We have no right to take the life of a fox for her coat, or a pig for his flesh, simply because our taste calls for it. Just as we would balk at testing drugs on unwilling human subjects, we must protest at the use of rats, rabbits and chimpanzees for similar purposes. These animals are as capable of suffering physical pain and psychological anguish as a human being. Our exploitation of other species for our own profit is as reprehensible as the exploitation of people of another race or sex.

'What kinds of experiments are performed?'

World-wide hundreds of millions of animals are subjected every year to experiments that blind, poison, mutilate, shock and burn them. Some tests last for hours at a time or continue over several days or years. Chimpanzees are kept for their lifetimes in AIDS and hepatitis studies; other primates languish in restraining devices for months. Small mammals used in product safety tests are force-fed toxic substances or have them dripped into their eyes. Dogs and cats discarded by their human companions may end up in vivisection labs.

'What can researchers use besides animals?'

Many alternatives to animal experiments exist, including clinical and epidemiological studies, cell and tissue cultures, mathematical, computer and mechanical models and audiovisual guides. Human patients with cancer, AIDS and other illnesses are often refused opportunities to try experimental treatments that offer some chance of success, and healthy volunteers are eager to participate in behavioural studies. The animals, however, have no choice, and anything can be (and is) done to them.

'Do animal experiments save lives?'

In countless cases animal experiments hurt, rather than help us. For example, potentially harmful chemicals are often kept on the market because animal test results are inconclusive. Substances that were tested on animals and determined 'safe' have caused dangerous side-effects when administered to human patients. While millions of animals die and billions are spent every year to confine them and make them sick, many people with crippling illnesses are unable to obtain adequate health care, drug and alcohol addiction treatment centres must turn away addicts for lack of funds and basic health care funding has been slashed to the bone.

'What's wrong with eating meat?'

The neatly wrapped packages in the meat case at the grocery store contain the body parts of animals who were raised in cramped quarters, unable to ever stretch a wing or take a few steps. They suffer from injuries and disease caused by overcrowding. By the time these animals reach the shops, more cows, pigs and chickens are being installed, like machines, on factory farms. They will continue through the macabre cycle that produces and kills 850 million animals a year in the UK. Although comparable in intelligence to dogs and other animals we keep as companions, these animals are never given the chance to play, to enjoy the sunshine or develop a living, natural relationship with others of their own kind. They never hear a warm word or feel a sensitive hand. With their needs and instincts thwarted and their lives cut short, animals raised for food are denied their right to live happily, for no better reason than our ugly habit (a taste for flesh) or desire for profit.

'What about nutrition?'

All meat, eggs and dairy products contain high concentrations of saturated fat and cholesterol, which have been irrefutably linked to heart disease, cancer and stroke, the three leading killers. Because animals raised on factory farms live in such unhealthy conditions, their feed, which often contains such cheap filler as cement dust, shredded newspaper and recycled animal wastes, is heavily laced with antibiotics, pesticides and hormones, the residues of which collect in the meat and are passed on to consumers. A vegetarian diet provides all the fibre and nutrition a person needs, without the ill effects of meat.

'Are animal rights good for the environment?'

Shockingly, the most devastating damage done to our planet stems from the production of meat and dairy products. Animal agriculture is very energy intensive. For example, animal farming is the UK's largest water user – 159 billion gallons each year. It takes 2,500 gallons of water to produce a pound of meat, but only 25 gallons to produce a pound of wheat, and a single processing plant may consume 100 million gallons of water daily. An animal-free diet saves trees too – an acre a year for each vegetarian. Animal grazing causes soil erosion and desertification and drains the earth's water reserves from aquifers.

Other forms of animal exploitation also wreak havoc on the earth. Hunting, trapping and 'sport' fishing disturb wildlife habitats with the presence of cars, equipment and dogs and upset the balance of animal populations by killing the largest, strongest and healthiest animals rather than those who are weak, old or sick, as nature would. Commercial fishing industries dump tons of plastic netting and rubbish into the oceans, polluting the waters and strangling and poisoning birds, fishes and marine mammals.

The capture of marine mammals for amusement parks and aquariums, of exotic birds for sale in pet shops, or of elephants and primates for zoos, circuses and research facilities tears animal families apart as well as their niches in nature. The animals who survive the harrowing journey to their final destination spend the rest of their lives in captivity, in conditions bearing little resemblance to the open spaces and infinite variety they are accustomed to.

© PETA

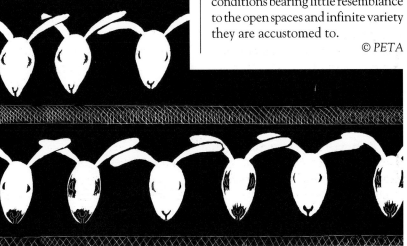

Is hunting cruel?

Information from the Countryside Alliance

In order to answer the question, 'Is hunting cruel?', one must first define cruelty. The Scott Henderson committee considered cruelty to be 'an act causing unnecessary suffering'.

There is no doubt that the fox population has to be controlled, and hunting with hounds is not only effective, but is also a method which involves minimal suffering. A fox which is hunted by a pack of hounds is either killed within seconds, or escapes entirely uninjured.

A popular myth is that the fox is killed by being torn apart by a pack of hounds when it is still alive. This is not true.

On average a foxhound weighs between 60 and 75 pounds, which makes it four or five times heavier than a fox. A fox is nearly always killed by a single bite to the back of the neck from just one foxhound's powerful jaws. This is irrespective of the number of hounds which might be in pursuit.

After a fox has been killed, the huntsman will often allow the pack to eat the corpse, but this is after the fox is dead.

Unlike those dogs which pursue their quarry by sight, fox hounds follow the scent of a fox – an invisible, intangible thread which hangs in the air or lies on the ground. They pick up the scent some time after the fox has been around, and for most of the pursuit are out of the fox's sight and hearing. Until the final stages, a fox is often quite unconcerned that it is being pursued at all.

As the Scott Henderson report put it: 'We are not satisfied that wild animals suffer from apprehension or the after-effects of fear to the same extent as human beings. Wild animals must live very largely in the present, and although a hunted fox, for example, may be aware that it is being hunted and that if the hounds catch it something to be avoided will happen, we think that it would be going beyond the evidence to say that the fox realises that it may be killed.'

The report continued: 'We think, therefore, that, while it is reasonable to assume that wild animals suffer from temporary fear and terror, there are no grounds for supposing that they suffer from apprehension to the same extent as human beings or that a frightening experience has the same serious or lasting effect upon them as it may have upon us.'

Even when it does realise that it is being followed, a fox will behave with great calm, almost to the point of indifference. It is certainly not terrified. Remember, this is a creature which is not itself in fear of predation. If it has been hunted by hounds before, it escaped unhurt. It has no reason to believe that it has anything to fear.

The majority of people who live in the countryside clearly believe, as evidenced by their public support of hunting and all its associated activities such as point-to-points and pony clubs, that the practice of foxhunting, controlled and under proper scrutiny, is the most acceptable method of controlling the fox population. Virtually all of these people keep and care about animals. It is difficult to accept that, in their hundreds of thousands, they would countenance, let alone actively support, anything which involved wanton cruelty.

And their support was borne out by the Scott Henderson committee: 'So far as general cruelty is concerned, we are satisfied that there is less cruelty in foxhunting than in most other methods of control. For that reason, and in view of the undisputed necessity for the control of foxes, we think that hunting should be allowed to continue. It is a necessary method of control, and its abolition would undoubtedly lead to an increase in the use of more cruel methods and, so far as we can judge, would be resented by the majority of the rural population.'

But key amongst the rural population are the farmers. It is they who allow the hunt to cross their land freely, for they appreciate the role which it plays in managing the fox population. The hunt is at all times responsive to their wishes.

A farmer who has experienced particular problems with foxes will often ask the hunt to kill a certain fox or to break up a group of foxes.

If a hunted fox goes to ground in a natural earth, the strictly-enforced rules of the governing body of foxhunting expressly prohibit the digging of the fox from the earth and continuing to hunt it. Nevertheless, a farmer will often insist that the fox, having been located by the hunt, is killed. Under such circumstances, trained staff who follow the hunt on foot are instructed to establish the whereabouts of the fox, to dig down to it, and to dispatch it instantly with a humane killer – usually a small pistol fired at point blank range.

These men will often use terriers to hold the fox at bay in a particular part of the earth. They go about their necessary work with all haste, and the fox is quickly destroyed. The sole purpose of digging is to kill a specific fox at the behest of the landowner. It is not any part of the sport of foxhunting. Farmers also expect families of foxes to be reduced in number and/or dispersed. This usually happens in the autumn, and the practice is called autumn hunting or cub-hunting. The word cub is something of a misnomer. These are families of foxes which may be in their first year, but have normally reached maturity.

At this time of year cattle are still out in the fields, and some crops have yet to be harvested. The hunt may therefore encircle a piece of woodland, into which foxhounds will be directed. The hounds and any foxes they find are encouraged to stay within the woodland, with two objectives.

The first is to ensure that a number of foxes are killed or dispersed. Dispersal results because those foxes which successfully break from cover scatter in all directions. The second is to develop the young hounds which have joined the pack during the summer. They have important lessons to learn. They must be taught to distinguish between, for example, foxes and deer, and only to hunt foxes; to know the sound of the horn and what the various calls mean. The huntsman uses his horn and his voice to communicate with his hounds in the way that a shepherd gives instructions to a sheepdog. The close constraints of a piece of woodland enable the huntsman to control the younger hounds and in this way to teach them. 'Holding up' as described above may only take place with the explicit instruction of the Hunt Master and at the request of the farmer or landowner, for fox control or farming reasons.

The importance of hunting to conservation

The British countryside is a man-made scene, not a natural one. Our rich heritage of fauna and flora has survived better than in any other European country because of the love

and dedication of generations of country people. For centuries country sports have played a central role in the process.

We can justly claim that many of the beautiful features of our landscape – the woods, spinneys, hedges, fields, lakes, streams, ponds, moors and heath are fashioned and preserved by the pattern of country sports.

As tens of thousands of country people contemplate a bleak future for agriculture, it is vital that all leisure and sporting activities rooted in the countryside are preserved.

The Farming and Wildlife Advisory Group recognises that hunting continues to make a significant contribution to conservation: 'The conservation element is inseparable from the provision of hunting . . .'

In the country of the Warwickshire Foxhounds, 55 woodland areas have been planted specifically for the purpose of hunting and of making coverts for foxes. Like many hunts, the Warwickshire owns some of these coverts – seven of them together span nearly 150 acres.

The hunt plays a large part in keeping local bridleways open, maintaining hedges and fences, and clearing and managing woodland. The hunt also encourages traditional laying of hedges and management of coverts, making an attractive habitat for wildlife of all kinds.

The importance of hunting to the rural economy

Over 7,000 people – professional hunt staff, terriermen, fence builders and stable staff – rely entirely on hunting for their full-time employment. It has been calculated that a further 8,900 people who work in the trades and professions associated with hunting – farriers, feed merchants, vets, saddlers, livery yards, bootmakers and so on – would lose their jobs if hunting were to be banned. So the employment generated by hunting is nearly 16,000 jobs. This does not take into account the knock-on effect of job losses in the indirectly dependent trades.

In a survey conducted by the Leicestershire Branch of the Blacksmiths' and Farriers' Association, half the respondents stated that without hunting they would not be able to continue in full-time practice during the winter, and the average anticipated loss of work was 50%.

Hunts have traditionally collected fallen stock from farmers. If this service ended, farmers would face higher charges from knackermen.

Hunting is deeply ingrained in rural life. Hunt supporters' clubs, some with over 1,500 members, bring together the rural community. Hunt point-to-points, puppy shows, supporters' club suppers, dances, horse trials and fund-raising events are central to the countryside calendar.

Hunt point-to-points are more popular than ever. Average crowds of nearly 4,000 exceed those of National Hunt meetings. All point-to-point horses must go hunting, which preserves the amateur basis of the sport and its place in the racing calendar.

A sport conducted under rules

All recognised packs of hounds are governed by one of the Masters of Hounds Associations, which impose strict rules on the sport. The cardinal law of hunting is expressed in Rule 1 of the Masters of Foxhounds Association. The other Associations have a similar rule:

'Foxhunting as a sport is the hunting of the fox in his wild and natural state with a pack of hounds. No pack of hounds, of which the Master or Representative is a Member of this Association, shall be allowed to hunt a fox in any way which is inconsistent with this precept.'

The sanctions are considerable, and could result in a hunt being closed down.

These rules ensure that all foxes are either humanely dispatched or escape without injury. No other method of control is regulated in this way. None can guarantee that foxes will escape unharmed.

Unlike other methods of control, hunting has a closed season. Unless they are causing a particular problem, efforts are made not to hunt or kill vixens when they are breeding and, between the end of April and late summer, hunting is suspended to allow young foxes to reach maturity.

Each hunt appoints a master or joint masters to run the 'country' – the area of land over which they hunt. This will on the whole be farmland, and it is with the farmers' express consent that the hunt will operate.

The master employs professional staff to look after the hounds. Only one person in the hunt is the huntsman, and he is responsible, with his assistants, the whippers-in, for hunting the quarry and controlling the hounds.

All other followers are there to enjoy the hunting. Some merely enjoy riding, running or walking. Most love to watch the hounds.

A sport with a following

From the very beginning, hunting has been open to all. It is not necessary to ride a horse to enjoy the sport. Large numbers of supporters follow on foot or by car. Research in 1995 showed that over 60% of the followers of the mounted packs were unmounted. Beagles, mink hounds, and the fell packs of foxhounds are all foot packs and cost as litle as one pound a day to follow.

As a result, hunting is as popular as ever, with over 200,000 people regularly taking part. Throughout Britain there are 185 packs of foxhounds, 9 packs of fell foxhounds, 71 packs of beagles, 19 packs of harriers, 10 packs of basset hounds, 19 packs of mink hounds and 3 packs of deer hounds. Despite amalgamations and losses of hunting country to urbanisation, there are more packs of hounds in Britain than in 1900.

Hunting gives its followers unparalleled access to the countryside, for it takes place with permission on millions of acres of private land. No other sport or recreation offers such an opportunity to ordinary people.

Hunting takes place with the consent and support of the overwhelming majority of farmers. For

example, the York and Ainsty North Foxhounds, a typical lowland pack, hunt over 99% of farms in their country; 75% of their subscribers being farmers or farmers' wives.

Hounds

The average hunt has 35 couples (i.e. 70) of hounds. Their ancestry can be traced back to 1800.

Hounds are working dogs. They cannot make family pets and are miserable if kept out of work or alone. Without hunting, the only humane choice would be to put down 20,000 foxhounds, harriers, beagles, basset and mink hounds. At a stroke, these hunting breeds would disappear forever.

In conclusion

The fox is a ruthless predator, one capable of inflicting great damage. No one disputes that fox numbers have to be controlled, and hunting is not only the most discriminating method of doing so, it is also the one which involves least cruelty.

Hunting has created and sustains many jobs in rural areas. It plays a vital role in shaping and protecting the British countryside.

It is true that those people who go hunting derive great pleasure from their sport, but it would be wrong to assume that what interests them is the death of an animal. Only the huntsman and his whippers-in are actually involved in the process of hunting the fox. The rest of the field are there to follow – on horseback, on foot or by car. Very few people indeed actually witness the death of a fox.

The followers are there for a day out in the countryside. An opportunity to ride or walk freely over private property with the consent of the landowner. To see the skill of man and animal working in tandem. To experience a part of life in the British countryside which has changed little over the centuries. One which deserves to survive for centuries to come.

• The above is an extract from the Countryside Alliance web site. See page 41 for address details.

© Countryside Alliance 1998

The facts about fox-hunting

Information from the RSPCA

The fox in history

The hunting of wild animals with dogs for sport has been a tradition in the UK for 1,000 years. Established by the Normans in the 11th century, this form of hunting was in its earliest days the 'sport of kings'. Forest and game laws protected the deer and wild boar which were the 'King's Beasts', and so severe were the penalties for their infringement that the ordinary man hunted at his peril.

Hares, red deer, wolves and wild boar – the 'Beasts of Venery' – were highly prized, and the fox was to find favour only later as an object of pursuit. Its popularity grew considerably, however, during the Civil War (1642-51), when the destruction of parks and forests harbouring deer reduced the numbers of this more desirable quarry.

By the 18th century, improved breeding in both hounds and horses to produce greater strength and stamina meant that hunts were able to travel many miles in pursuit of foxes, which were destroyed in large numbers.

With the sport's continuation, therefore, under threat for lack of quarry, it was vital to increase the fox population. Animals were imported from the Continent, and Leadenhall Market became a busy centre for fox trading.

The imported foxes were called 'bagmen', and were either released in hunt areas or kept in hunt kennels to supply demand as necessary. Occasionally the bagmen were recaptured by their pursuers and returned to their kennels to be chased again another day.[1]

The late 1700s saw the beginning of major changes in the English landscape following the passing of the Enclosure Acts. As open areas of land began to be enclosed and arable farming spread, landowners in the big hunting counties of Leicestershire, Northamptonshire and Warwickshire set aside areas where foxes could breed. This ensured that their number remained high enough for hunting to continue.

By the early 19th century, foxhunting had become a favourite sport of country landowners, and it has continued into the 20th century as a widespread country pursuit.

The hunt

The requirements of the hunt followers for a 'successful' hunt are foxes to pursue (but not so many that the hounds are distracted from keeping to a line) and a chase which is as long as possible.

The opening meet of the season is generally held early in November. To ensure a long chase, and to make certain that there are foxes to be found in the open immediately after the meet, 'earth stoppers' are employed to close up earths (and badger setts, in which foxes may try to take refuge) during the night before or early in the morning of a hunting day.

Many hunts maintain artificial earths to ensure a sufficient supply of foxes for hunting through the season, and a quarter of all hunts have more than 12 such earths.[2] The fox is therefore prevented from returning to its earth after a night's feeding and from taking refuge too soon to give the hunt a 'good chase'.

Hunting does not begin until after 11am to allow the fox time to digest its night's intake of food and to ensure that it is capable of a long, hard run. A day's hunting is regarded as 'good' when it produces at least one fox that runs hard for an hour or more.

Such prolonged chases are unnatural for foxes and may therefore result in suffering. Recent research on red deer concluded that lengthy chases with hounds imposed stresses that are likely to cause great suffering.[3] Although the results for deer may not necessarily apply in foxes we should assume that they do until there is evidence to the contrary.

A fox which is run to ground may be left alone, or it may be dug out, taking perhaps several hours. Alternatively, terriers may be used to pursue it underground. This form of baiting may cause considerable suffering to both fox and dogs. Once the fox is forced to the surface, it may be killed or made to bolt to renew the chase.

Whether or not the fox is dug out depends on a number of factors:

the wishes of local farmers; the supply of foxes in the area; the feelings of the hunt followers; and the number of earths in the area.

Cub hunting is carried out in the autumn before the start of the hunting season, beginning usually in August or September, and serves to introduce new hounds to their job. The object is not to chase the young foxes, but to kill them in covert, and members of the hunt attend only by specific invitation of the Master of Foxhounds. Cubbing is not an activity in which the general public are invited to share.

Is the fox a pest?

One of the arguments most frequently used by supporters of fox-hunting is that the fox is a pest which needs to be controlled. This argument may take several forms.

For example, they may say that ' . . . the Countryman knows that a large number of foxes have to be killed',[4] or 'the Ministry of Agriculture, Fisheries and Food state that the fox is a pest to agriculture . . . '.[5] such statements suggest that those in authority most closely concerned with the countryside and agriculture regard the fox as a pest and, therefore, it must be so.

In fact, there is no list of officially classified mammalian pests. There is, however, a reference in the Agriculture Act 1947 to foxes as one of the species against which the Ministry may require a landowner to take action if, for example, they are damaging livestock.

Since the passage of that Act, however, many scientific studies have been carried out on the fox and it is interesting to compare their findings with traditional beliefs about fox predation. It is also interesting to note that much of the research has been undertaken by scientific staff of government agricultural departments.

The introduction to a scientific paper[6] began by commenting that 'much of the case against foxes as pests of agriculture in Scotland stems from the finding of lamb carcasses at fox dens. It is often assumed by farmers and shepherds that these represent predated viable lambs . . . but many lambs are taken as carrion.'

Scientific investigations which have sought to differentiate between scavenging on dead lambs and sheep and predation on live lambs have clearly indicated that, while foxes may take large quantities of carrion, the actual loss of live lambs to foxes is very low indeed.

In many areas, carrion is widely available in addition to prey such as rabbits and small rodents. An indication of just how much carrion there may be comes from one study area, a large Scottish estate on which some 700 blackface sheep over-wintered on the open hill.[7]

Lambing took place in late April in hill parks. Ewe mortality was about six per cent (an average figure for this sort of holding) and about two-thirds of it occurred from March to May. It yielded an abundance of carrion which was not fully exploited by foxes or any other animals. This source of food was increased by lambs which were stillborn or which died soon after birth.

Further evidence has come from investigations by the Ministry of Agriculture, Fisheries and Food.[8] During 1983, a study was carried out in an upland/hill area of Powys stocked with 3,500 lambing ewes. Foxes were present in the area, but lamb losses were found to be unaffected by foxes. It might be argued that predation of lambs would be worse without control measures against the fox. But it is an interesting fact that on the island of Mull, where there are no foxes, lamb production is no better than in comparable areas of Scotland where foxes are present.[9] A study comparing lamb losses in areas with and without fox control found no evidence of an increase in fox predation on lambs in the absence of control.[10] It is, therefore, difficult to argue that fox predation makes substantial inroads into the production of lambs.

However, between three and four million lambs are lost each year as a result of factors such as exposure and starvation, and management should be aimed at reducing this major cause of lamb loss on hill farms.[11]

Another aspect of the argument against the fox as a pest concerns the killing of poultry. Birds that are

housed are however at little risk from foxes, and though free-range birds are potentially at greater risk, they can be effectively protected by strong or electrified fencing.[12]

If birds are vulnerable to attack by foxes, it is usually because they are inadequately protected, and closer attention to husbandry practices is likely to resolve the problem.

Controlling the fox?

Studies by biologists over the past 30 years have provided much new information about the behaviour and biology of foxes, which should be borne in mind when considering measures to control either individual animals or populations.

For example, it has been shown that fox 'society' is complex. In some areas, foxes may live in groups generally composed of one dog fox and several vixens. Usually only the dominant vixen in the group produces cubs, which the remaining vixens help to guard and rear.

It is clear, therefore, that reproduction in these subservient females is socially suppressed, though the mechanism by which this system works is not yet fully understood.[13]

It is equally clear that so-called 'control' measures like hunting are likely to disrupt such a social system and may result in more vixens producing cubs.[14]

The RSPCA has supported scientific studies of foxes, but more work has still to be done on aspects of fox biology to understand more fully the biological consequences of manipulating fox populations. It is obvious, however, that specific problems require specific solutions and, while it may occasionally be necessary to take action against an individual problem animal, 'war' on the species as a whole cannot be justified.

The fox and conservation

In recent years there has been a growing awareness of many environmental problems and of the urgent need to conserve wildlife and habitats. Not surprisingly, supporters of fox-hunting have allied themselves with this cause.

It is, for example, often stated that farmers and landowners who support hunting plant and preserve hedgerows and coverts, and that in the absence of fox-hunting such habitats would be removed.

This assertion rests on a number of questionable assumptions. For instance, trees and woodland have a variety of purposes on farmland, such as landscaping and general amenity, wildlife conservation and shelter or screening. The importance that a farmer or landowner attaches to these purposes will vary.

It is, however, interesting to note that in a survey carried out by the Ministry of Agriculture, Fisheries and Food,[15] farmers generally considered that game, hunting and shooting were only minor benefits as far as woods and trees were concerned. The survey was extensive, covering 1 million hectares (approximately $2\frac{1}{2}$ million acres) of farmland throughout England and Wales, and may therefore be regarded as representative of farmers' views.

A survey of members of the Timber Growers' Organisation also indicated that providing coverts for foxes ranked bottom of the list regarding motives for retaining or planting small woods.[16]

Such results clearly undermine considerably the hunt supporters' argument that without fox-hunting, farmers would destroy more hedgerows and copses.

The humane alternative

Supporters of fox-hunting claim that 'what the field enjoys is not the kill (which it rarely sees) but the working with hounds, and the taking of a line across country wherever the fox may lead and whatever the obstacles, hazards and uncertainties'.[17]

If that is so, ample opportunity for such enjoyment should be provided by the sport of drag hunting, in which the riders and dogs follow a specially laid trail instead of a live animal.

Not only can this alternative sport provide an exhilarating test for rider, horse and hound, but it offers the security of continued employment to the saddlers, tailors, horse breeders and others whose livelihoods would, it is said by hunt-supporters, be jeopardised by the abolition of fox-hunting.

References
1. *The Red Fox*. H.G. Lloyd (1980) Batsford Ltd, London.
2. *The Politics of Hunting*. R.H. Thomas (1983) Gower Publishing Company Ltd, Aldershot.
3. *The Behavioural and Physiological Effects of Culling Red Deer*. P. Bateson (1997) Report to the National Trust.
4. *This is Foxhunting*. Anon (1978) British Field Sports Society.
5. *Country Sports Do You Really Know the Facts?* Anon. The Campaign for Country Sports.
6. Lamb Carcasses and Other Food Remains at Fox Dens in Scotland. R. Hewson (1985) *Notes from the Mammal Society*, No 50, pp 291-296.
7. The Food of Foxes in Forests and on the Open Hill. R. Hewson and A.F. Leitch (1983) *Scottish Forestry* 37, pp 39-50.
8. *Research and Development Report: Mammal and Bird Pests* 1983. Anon (1985) Ministry of Agriculture, Fisheries and Food, No 255 (83).
9. Scavenging and Predation upon Sheep and Lambs in West Scotland. R. Hewson (1984) *Journal of Applied Ecology* 21, pp 843-868.
10. *Predation upon lambs by foxes in the absence of control*. R. Hewson (1990) Report to the League Against Cruel Sports.
11. Lamb mortality on a hill farm. B.G. Merrell (1995) *Proceedings of the Sheep Veterinary Society*, pp21-25.
12. *Protecting poultry from predators*. (1987) ADAS, Ministry of Agriculture, Fisheries and Food.
13. Fox Family Planning. Chapter 8 in *Running with the fox*. D. Macdonald (1987) Unwin Hyman.
14. The control of canid populations. S. Harris and G. Saunders (1993) *Symp. Zool. Soc. Lond.* 65, pp 441-464.
15. Survey of Environmental Topics on Farms England and Wales: 1985. Anon (1985) Ministry of Agriculture, Fisheries and Food, *Statistical Notice* No 244/85.
16. *Countryside Sports; Their Economic And Conservation Significance*. Cobham Resource Consultants (1992) The standing conference on countryside sports.
17. *Field Sports and Wildlife in the United Kingdom: A Statement*. Anon (1978) British Field Sports Society.

Country sports

Focus on the figures

In 1996:
- 3.3 million people went fishing
- 704,000 people shot game and wildfowl
- 14,500 people stalked deer
- 215,500 people hunted or followed hounds
- 12,500 people participated in falconry

This relates to approximately 130 million activity days in recreation and leisure.

Annual direct expenditure on country sports was over £3.8 billion.

This spending generated direct employment equivalent to 60,150 full-time jobs.

Direct employment generated by game fishing, shooting and stalking in Scotland is estimated at approximately 2,950 full-time job equivalents.

The sports contributed produce for sale valued for sale wholesale at:
- £12-18 million game
- £0.65 million fish
- £9.0 million venison

Government income from taxes, licences, rates, etc. was £655 million

All figures from *Countryside Sports – their Economic, Social and Conservation Significance* by Cobham Resource Consultants for Standing Conference on Countryside Sports, 1997.

Fox-hunting

Banning this might sound like a good idea . . . but for every fox killed by the hunt, 20 die in other ways

- 10,000 foxes killed by lurchers.
- 80,000 foxes shot.
- 100,000 foxes killed on the roads.
- 30,000 foxes snared.
- 110,000 foxes die of natural causes and by unknown means.*
- 50,000 foxes killed by terriers outside organised hunting.

All figures are approximations.
* Up to 40,000 foxes die of natural causes. Shooting, snaring, terrier work or illegal gassing and poisoning probably account for the rest.

Putting the fox first

For most people fox-hunting is a black and white issue. It is either entirely right or entirely wrong, and virtually everyone has an opinion about it, whether informed or not. Today fox-hunting is more contentious than ever and many believe a ban is imminent.

But where would that leave the fox? Most probably, worse off. Other methods, some more cruel and unaccountable, are likely to replace hunting.

So should we leave hunting well alone? The simple answer is no. Wildlife Network believes that for the fox's sake, hunting with hounds should be reformed, not banned.

Wildlife Network was created by former leaders of the League Against Cruel Sports who came to realise that an all-out ban on fox-hunting could make life worse for the fox, not better.

Is the fox a pest?

Most farmers – especially hill farmers with sheep – would say yes, the fox is a pest.

There is no doubt that foxes do cause localised problems, but scientific studies suggest that taken overall, foxes are no more than a minor nuisance nationally. Hypothermia and poor stockmanship are bigger killers of lambs than foxes ever were.

However, if landowners and farmers believe that foxes are vermin

– and banning hunts will do nothing to change that perception – they will continue to kill them or have them killed. Indeed, the number of foxes shot and snared is already five times greater than the number killed by hunts. Traditional hunting is as much a check on ruthless and more cruel methods of slaughter as it is a check on the fox.

Hunting with hounds is far from efficient. Last year, for example, the average lowland hunt killed 80-100 foxes. By comparison, a single sheep farmer in the Mendip Hills shoots over 40 foxes a year; a gun pack in Wales can kill over 20 foxes on a day's shoot; and a terrier gang, operating independently of the hunt, can kill up to 100 foxes a year.

Many farmers in hunting areas tolerate the fox precisely because it is hunted, giving them and others sport, and because they feel that hunting helps to control the fox population. Ban the hunt and many farmers and landowners may well allow increased fox-killing by whatever means, fair or foul.

Not a black and white issue

There is no love lost between the traditional hunts controlled by the Masters of Foxhounds Association and the shady end of the fox-killing business – the unpoliced gangs of hard men with hard dogs who revel in digging out and killing foxes.

Unfortunately, the strident and uncompromising campaign to abolish hunting has driven them into an uneasy alliance. Wildlife Network believes it is time to sort the tolerable practices from the intolerable.

There are two things which can happen to a hunted fox. It can escape or it can be killed. Death in the mouths of the hounds is gruesome, but far more worrying is the fate of those foxes – an estimated 10,000 – which are dug out by the hunt terriermen once they have gone to ground. At its worst, this practice can lead to terriers tormenting and attacking foxes underground for hours before they are finally killed. Even the dogs can be severely wounded or killed.

So why not ban terrier work? In an ideal world we would – but the world is not ideal and realism must guide us here. For most farmers and landowners, fox-hunting is a mixture of several things: sport for riders and

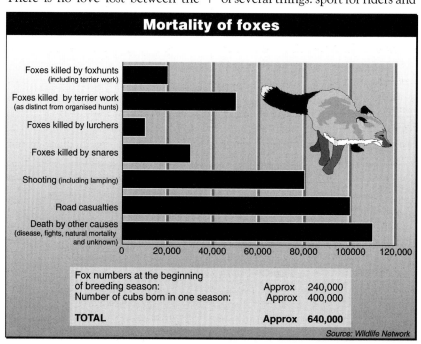

Mortality of foxes

Foxes killed by foxhunts (including terrier work)	
Foxes killed by terrier work (as distinct from organised hunts)	
Foxes killed by lurchers	
Foxes killed by snares	
Shooting (including lamping)	
Road casualties	
Death by other causes (disease, fights, natural mortality and unknown)	

(scale: 0, 20,000, 40,000, 60,000, 80,000, 100,000, 120,000)

Fox numbers at the beginning of breeding season:	Approx	240,000
Number of cubs born in one season:	Approx	400,000
TOTAL	**Approx**	**640,000**

Source: Wildlife Network

followers, a rural tradition of long standing and a form of pest control. Ban terrier work and hunting would be seen by many farmers – the majority in some areas – as next to useless as a means of fox control. And that could lead to more shooting, more snaring, greater cruelty and quite possibly a higher annual death toll. Some people say that if this is the case, then the shooting and snaring of foxes should be banned. But that is simply not going to happen.

The way forward

Wildlife Network recognises that some farmers and landowners will want terrier work to remain available to them as an option for fox control.

However, it believes that both terrier work and the whole business of hunting with hounds must be brought under strict, independent control.

- Wildlife Network calls upon the Government to establish an independent authority to regulate and oversee the hunting of foxes. Animal welfare groups should be represented on this new watch-dog, alongside experts from the worlds of hunting, science, farming and conservation.
- Hunts should operate only under licence granted by the new authority.
- The activity of cub-hunting should be ended and the proper fox-hunting season should start at the beginning of October.
- In order that nursing vixens are not hunted, the fox-hunting season should end no later than mid-March.
- Unless requested by the land-owner or farmer, the digging out of foxes should be illegal.
- Terrier work should be allowed only under licence, likewise granted by the same authority.

The following conditions should apply:
- The use of hard (baiting) dogs should be forbidden, and terrier men should only use dogs which stand off from the located fox and do not attack it.
- Foxes should be killed with a .22 pistol or other appropriate calibre weapon.

- Terriers should spend no more than one hour underground.
- The intention should be to bolt the fox into a net in order that it can be immediately shot.
- The terrier must wear a locator in order that its position under-ground can always be tracked.
- The use of dogs such as lurchers to hunt and kill foxes should be made illegal.
- Wildlife Network believes the Government should review the Wildlife and Countryside Act (1981) to examine all aspects of controlling and killing wildlife, including the use of snares. There is an urgent need for independent and impartial research and analysis of these complex issues.

- If you would like an application form to become a supporter of Wildlife Network, please write to: Wildlife Network, Mowbray Lodge, 6 Catmos Street, Oakham, Rutland LE15 6HW or telephone 01572 771355.

© Wildlife Network
August, 1998

Animal rights and wrongs

The RSPCA's withdrawal of its long-standing statement support-ing 'animal rights' is a welcome move, but one taken reluctantly, to avoid falling foul of rules governing charities. The RSPCA is no longer devoted to preventing needless and deplorable cruelty, but a pressure group of animal rights activists that follows the views of the Australian philosopher Peter Singer and the notion of 'speciesism' developed by Richard Ryder, a former chairman.

There should be no hesitation in properly describing this as a completely immoral view. The arguments of Singer and Ryder, which rest on casuistry and simplified exhortations, take no account of key ethical principles examined by philosophers from Aristotle and Kant to the present day. Rights are accompanied by the capacity to make moral choices and accept obligations.

Animals live in the present unaware of their own mortality, without making moral or aesthetic judge-ments, and without responsibilities or duties.

Although they are not moral beings, we are, and should not inflict needless suffering – not because of their inherent rights, but because it demonstrates a failing in our own moral compass.

Sentiment has its place in our dealings with animals. Few who oppose fox-hunting object to cats hunting mice. Cats (and dogs and horses) engage our sympathies: the same cannot be said of cockroaches, slugs or rats. This distinction may be arbitrary, but it is foolish to ignore it. It ensures the survival of animals in which human beings take an interest. Were they not hunted, deer, grouse and pheasants would be less common.

The pleasure afforded by fox-hunting or angling does not lie in the suffering of the animal, but in the sport itself. To follow the RSPCA's doctrines on rights would result in outlawing any activity which offers pleasure bought at a cost to animals. That would abolish most of cookery, as well as racing, shooting, hunting and fishing.

The Christian view of animals, framed as much by St Francis as St Thomas Aquinas, follows the scriptural instruction that man should have dominion over the beasts of the field. That good husbandry has brought benefits to both. The move towards a vegan society which prohibits all sport, medical experi-ments, or food which involves animals, logically required by animal rights, would lead to suffering for humans and animals alike.

© Telegraph Group Limited,
London 1998

This is foxhunting

Information from the Countryside Alliance

Foxhunting is the pursuit of the wild fox with a pack of hounds. Man has been controlling foxes since he started to farm animals, but the hunting of foxes with hounds for sport became popular over two hundred years ago.

The fox is a pest and its population needs to be controlled. Individuals and organisations concerned with farming and the management of the countryside recognise this fact. Responsible fox management includes maintaining a healthy population at a level at which it can thrive without threatening livestock or other wildlife.

Foxhunting is the most natural method of management: by its nature, it takes out the old, sick and injured foxes, and there is no risk of wounding. If the fox is caught, it is killed within seconds. If the fox goes to ground, it will either be left unharmed or the landowner may ask that it be killed by the hunt's terrierman. The strict rules governing terrier work laid down by the Masters of Fox Hounds Association (MFHA) ensure there is no unnecessary suffering.

Foxhunting does not just help control fox numbers. Landowners with an interest in foxhunting plant and maintain coverts, woodlands and copses for the benefit of all wildlife. Few farmers want to see the fox exterminated, but those who support hunting are more inclined to tolerate foxes on their land, as long as their numbers are controlled.

The fox

In rural areas of the UK, the red fox is in very good shape. After two hundred years of organised hunting, it is a well-conserved species. The British fox commands respect, but should not command sentimentality.

Being an opportunist predator, the fox will kill poultry, wildfowl, newborn lambs and piglets beyond the needs of its staple diet of small wild mammals, insects and worms.

The fox is a hunter and covers considerable distances hunting for food or in search of a mate. Like all wild animals when threatened, the fox attempts to put an adequate 'flight distance' between itself and a potential enemy. This is a natural survival instinct.

Hunting the fox

Each hunt has its own designated area called the hunt country. The hunt meets at a predetermined place and moves off to a 'draw', a particular woodland or other habitat where foxes are likely to be found.

The only people involved with the hunting of the fox are the huntsman and his assistants, called Whippers-In. Mounted followers (the Field), under the control of the Field Master, are kept far enough away from the hounds to ensure they can work unhindered. Between 30 and 40 hounds (15 and 20 'couples') hunt on a given day.

Hounds are bred for intelligence, speed, stamina, voice and 'nose' (sense of smell). They follow the scent of a fox, which may be quite some distance away. When the fox is killed, the pack will often eat the corpse. This has led to the false belief that the hounds tear a live fox to pieces. This is a myth.

Seasons

Hunting is the only form of fox control that recognises a closed season.

Autumn hunting: August/September – October

Foxes may be less than a year old but are, by this time, fully grown, and living and hunting independently. The objectives of autumn hunting are to cull some foxes and to disperse others, ensuring there are not too many in one area. Hounds hunt by instinct but during this period they learn to hunt only foxes.

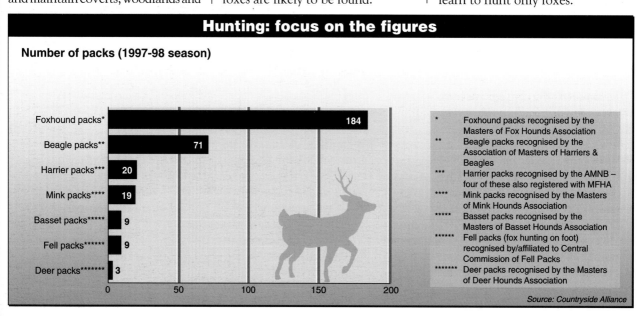

Hunting: focus on the figures

Number of packs (1997-98 season)

Pack	Number
Foxhound packs*	184
Beagle packs**	71
Harrier packs***	20
Mink packs****	19
Basset packs*****	9
Fell packs******	9
Deer packs*******	3

*   Foxhound packs recognised by the Masters of Fox Hounds Association
**   Beagle packs recognised by the Association of Masters of Harriers & Beagles
***   Harrier packs recognised by the AMNB – four of these also registered with MFHA
**** Mink packs recognised by the Masters of Mink Hounds Association
***** Basset packs recognised by the Masters of Basset Hounds Association
****** Fell packs (fox hunting on foot) recognised by/affiliated to Central Commission of Fell Packs
******* Deer packs recognised by the Masters of Deer Hounds Association

Source: Countryside Alliance

Foxhunting: November – March/April
The duration of the season varies according to the nature of the farming in the area.

Call-outs: usually spring
A farmer who is losing lambs, piglets or poultry may ask the hunt to track and kill the guilty fox. This is responsible work, not sport.

'There is no doubt . . . that foxes can be damaging and indiscriminate predators of birds and other animals . . . Control methods must remain available to those suffering economic damage from foxes.' (Labour Party policy document, *Wildlife in the Countryside*, 1991)

Questions and answers

Surely, a ban on hunting would benefit the fox?
'The trouble is that people see pictures of cowering foxes, feel sympathy for the fox, and then immediately conclude that foxhunting should be banned. There's no real thought about what effect such a ban would in fact have on foxes. Of course, what would happen would be that far more would be shot, trapped and gassed.' (Jim Barrington, former Executive Director of the League Against Cruel Sports)

Is the case for fox control overstated?
No. Fox predation causes significant lamb losses. Scientific estimates vary from 0.5% to 5.2%. Even at 2%, the cost to a typical hill farmer with 1,500 ewes is over £1,000. Without control, predation would increase considerably.

What would be the consequences of a ban on foxhunting?
15,900 people whose jobs directly depend on foxhunting would be out of work. Some 14,000 foxhounds would have no future as these working pack dogs would not make suitable pets. There would be less incentive for farmers to conserve wildlife habitat.

Is draghunting an alternative to foxhunting?
No. The Masters of Draghounds

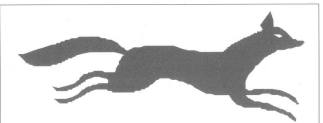

Association states: 'We strongly refute claims that draghunting is an alternative to foxhunting. Draghunting is an exciting equestrian sport in its own right, but is totally different to any other type of hound sport. It plays no role in the management of the red fox, which many farmers regard as a pest.'

Is foxhunting a popular sport?
Yes. There are 194 registered packs of foxhounds in the UK followed by more than 50,000 riders and over 110,000 foot or car followers.

Come foxhunting
If you would like to follow a hunt, contact the Countryside Alliance for assistance. Foot followers may be asked to pay a daily 'cap' of £1 or £2.

Mounted followers pay between £25 and £70 per day. Some hunts run 'Newcomer Days' as an introduction to the sport for a minimal fee.

Foot followers should wear warm and waterproof clothing. Correct dress for mounted followers can vary and the Hunt Secretary should be consulted in advance of your first visit.

Code of Conduct
Foxhunting is controlled by the Masters of Fox Hounds Association, which has strong sanctions to enforce its rules. Each hunt has Masters who are responsible for organising hunting, and ensuring that the MFHA Rules and the Code of Conduct are followed. Hunting depends on the goodwill of farmers who welcome the hunt, and followers must behave accordingly.
• The above is an extract from the Countryside Alliance web site. See page 41 for address details.

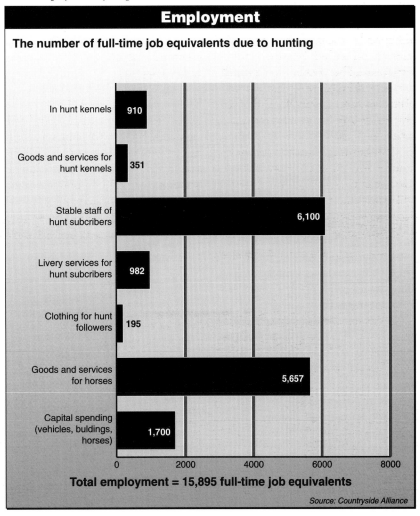

Employment
The number of full-time job equivalents due to hunting

Category	Full-time job equivalents
In hunt kennels	910
Goods and services for hunt kennels	351
Stable staff of hunt subcribers	6,100
Livery services for hunt subcribers	982
Clothing for hunt followers	195
Goods and services for horses	5,657
Capital spending (vehicles, buldings, horses)	1,700

Total employment = 15,895 full-time job equivalents

Source: Countryside Alliance

This is draghunting

Information from the Countryside Alliance

Draghunting is an exciting, non-competitive cross-country equestrian sport, guaranteed to provide a lot of galloping and jumping. Drag hound packs use foxhounds that are trained to hunt a man dragging an enhanced scent. The other form of draghunting, often described as 'hunting the clean boot', uses bloodhounds, which have a very keen scenting nose and follow the natural scent of a human runner.

The hunting day is organised by the hunt Line Managers, with the permission of the landowner or farmer over whose land the day's sport is arranged. The farmer determines over which part of the land he wishes the hunt to run. The Line Manager tries to use as much of the natural countryside as practical, such as hedges, ditches, rivers and walls. If there are not enough natural obstacles to jump, the hunt may build their own fences, or use portable jumps.

Often the draghunt day will incorporate an existing hunter trial course as part of a line. The name of the game is to jump as many obstacles as possible whilst following the drag hounds or bloodhounds.

The hounds

Drag hounds are usually foxhounds, given to the drag hound pack by their local pack of foxhounds. The scent dragged by the runner or rider who lays the 'line' is strong, allowing the hounds to travel very fast across country. The bloodhound packs use a purpose-bred, athletic type of bloodhound, which only needs a short sniff of an article of clothing belonging to their quarry. The bloodhound has the most acute sense of smell of any member of the dog or hound breeds, but is one of the most difficult to handle within a pack environment, due to the individuality of each hound.

The hunt

Each hunt has its own hunt 'country'. Because draghunting requires a larger area to set up its day, most packs have at least two registered foxhound packs within their country.

The hunting day can involve anything from 3-6 lines; each line may be from 1-5 miles long. The country and roads dictate the line distance.

There may be anywhere from six to thirty jumps in each line, and the day may be made up of three to six lines. A four to six-line day requires a very fit horse and rider.

Different packs set up their days to suit their followers' abilities and inclination. Many hunts cater for the novice rider, and the non-jumpers as well as for the more confident rider.

Seasons

Like all forms of mounted hunting, draghunting takes place through the autumn, winter and early spring, depending on the weather and local farming conditions.

Questions and answers

Is draghunting an alternative to foxhunting?
No. Draghunting requires a much larger area, and there is not enough country available for all the foxhound packs to turn to draghunting. They are completely different sports.

Is draghunting becoming more popular?
Yes. Competition riders find that draghunting complements their equestrian preparation, and fits in with limited spare time. For some,

the uncertainty is one of the attractions of foxhunting; those who want to be sure of a good day with plenty of galloping and jumping, prefer draghunting.

Is there more to draghunting than just riding and jumping across country?
Of course – the sport attracts many spectators who enjoy watching the action and because the lines are arranged, it is easy to find a good vantage point. All packs support a range of social activities, and for those particularly interested in hound work, the bloodhounds are of particular interest.

What is the difference between draghunting and 'hunting the clean boot' with bloodhounds?
The fundamental difference is the type of hound used. The bloodhound hunts only the natural scent of man, and particularly when scenting conditions are bad, will be noticeably slower than the hounds hunting the stronger artificial scent.

Come draghunting

If you would like to follow a draghunt or bloodhound pack, contact the Countryside Alliance for details of your nearest pack. A few packs are private, or subscription only, but most welcome visitors and occasional mounted followers will be asked to pay a 'cap' of between £25 and £50, depending on the hunt.

Foot followers should wear warm and waterproof clothing. Correct dress for mounted followers can vary and the Hunt Secretary should be consulted in advance of your first visit.

Code of conduct

The sport is administered and regulated by the Masters of Drag-hounds & Bloodhounds Association, Stable Cottage, Wheatsheaf Road, Hanfield, West Sussex.

© Countryside Alliance 1998

Draghunting – 'A family sport'

Information from the League Against Cruel Sports (LACS)

It is often claimed that the majority of people who ride to hounds are not interested in killing animals; in other words they 'hunt to ride' and don't 'ride to hunt'.

There are 12 registered drag hunts and 10 bloodhound packs already operating successfully in Britain. Drag hunts use fox hounds and the fact that the Oxford Drag Hunt uses hounds borrowed from the Bicester with Whaddon Chase Fox Hunt is proof that the hounds currently hunting foxes could be retrained to hunt the 'drag'.

It is no more difficult to train a hound to follow the scent of the 'drag' than it is to train it to follow the scent of a fox, hare or deer.

'The vast majority of farmers will not permit draghunting on their land.' – Janet George, BFSS, BBC Radio 5 Live, 3rd January '96.

The British Field Sports Society claims that the 'vast majority' of farmers welcome hunting on their land and pours scorn on the argument that draghunting (in which an artificial trail is laid across the countryside for hounds and rider to follow) could replace the hunting of foxes and other wild animals with hounds. The BFSS repeatedly claims that the reason farmers allow fox-hunts access to their land is because they want foxes killed.

The League Against Cruel Sports commissioned NOP to conduct a survey of farmers in an effort to establish whether draghunting is a viable alternative to fox-hunting and similar bloodsports.

NOP conducted the poll of 1,000 free-holding farmers between 8th and 19th March 1996. All areas, sizes and types of farm were covered.

The results prove that the claims of the British Field Sports Society are totally false!

Firstly, nearly half of Britain's farmers do not allow hunting on their land. If the hunting of foxes and other wild animals with hounds was outlawed by Parliament, the amount of farmland available to draghunting could be more than three-quarters of the amount on which hunting currently takes place. Drag hunts need much less hunting territory than fox hunts and because the 'trail' is pre-planned and controlled, can operate much more safely than fox-hunts near built-up areas, roads and railway lines. Certainly some farmers who currently allow fox hunting would not allow access to drag hunts. However, one in six farmers who do not currently allow the hunting of wild animals would permit access to drag hunts. Consequently, despite the loss of some existing hunting country as a result of a ban on fox-hunting and similar bloodsports, there would still be ample territory available for the 300 existing Hunts to switch to draghunting and each obtain access to farmland the equivalent in size to 300 times the size of London's St James's Park!

The advantages of a prohibition of hunting wild animals with dogs would be:
1) an end to the cruelty of hounding wild animals to exhaustion and death.
2) an increase in the number of Hunts, with greater public participation.

3) increased rural employment.
4) an end to protests and clashes between hunt supporters and saboteurs.
5) a reduction in policing and court costs.
6) an end to hounds causing road and rail accidents, damaging crops and gardens, stampeding livestock and killing family pets.

Hunt havoc

Every year, there are hundreds of incidents in which the hunted animal, such as a fox, in its desperate race for survival, leads the hounds over main roads and railway lines, through vulnerable crops, nature reserves, livestock and even into housing estates and private gardens. Inevitably on numerous such occasions the hounds riot and attack farm animals and poultry, kill family pet dogs and cats, cause road accidents, and stop intercity trains. Hounds are killed on roads and railway lines every season.

When hunting with drag hounds or bloodhounds, the trail is set avoiding all such hazards. Draghunting provides the thrill of the chase, but reduces the risk to horse and rider associated with jumping blindly over hedges and other obstacles which may conceal dangerous ditches or farm implements. And, to the benefit of riders and passing traffic, the trail can be laid so that the 'hunt' ends near the point it started. This avoids the danger associated with riders hacking back miles along unlit country lanes to return to their parked horseboxes.

• The above is an extract from *Draghunting – 'A family sport'*, produced by the League Against Cruel Sports (LACS)

Companion animals

People have been living with animals as companions for thousands of years. The ancient Egyptians, for example, were sharing their homes with cats and dogs 5,000 years ago. They even worshipped them as gods and had them preserved and buried in special animal cemeteries when they died!

Introduction

The ancestors of today's domestic dog were wild wolves and foxes. They probably began scavenging around early human settlements and, over time, started to substitute the human family for their own pack. Early people found that dogs were very useful and began to selectively breed and modify the species. They created breeds of dogs to help them hunt and guard their homes and livestock. Today, over half the households in Britain own a pet. There are about 7.2 million cats, 6.5 million dogs, 1.4 million rabbits and 0.9 million hamsters. We are certainly a nation of 'animal keepers', but do we deserve our reputation of 'animal lovers'?

The unloved

We pride ourselves on being a nation that cares passionately about animals. Yet every year thousands of perfectly healthy animals are destroyed simply because they are unwanted.

In 1995, the RSPCA destroyed or found homes for over 150,000 animals who had been abandoned or neglected by their owners. And it's not just the RSPCA who deal with unwanted pets. In a 1989 report, the RSPCA estimated that about 1,000 dogs are needlessly destroyed every day, by vets, other animal welfare organisations, the police and local authorities.

They also estimated that there are probably around $1/_2$ million stray and unwanted dogs roaming Britain's streets. Many pets are bought on a whim and then 'dumped' when their owners get bored with them or they become too much trouble. Often people simply don't appreciate what the cost of feeding and vet bills will be. At Christmas and holiday times animal rescue centres are usually full of animals dumped by owners who are going away and don't want the hassle of taking their pets with them, or the expense of boarding them.

The pet trade

People are often upset when they see animals displayed in pet shops. In fact, many animal groups such as Animal Aid and the RSPCA argue that it is wrong to sell animals in pet shops because it encourages people to 'impulse buy'. When people see a rabbit, kitten or puppy for sale they may be tempted to buy on the spot without thinking it through properly.

Pet shops aren't good places for animals. In 1990, a nation-wide survey of 100 pet shops by the *Which?* consumer magazine found that many animals were kept in over-crowded cages and in unsuitable conditions. They also found that staff often didn't know how to look after the animals they were selling!

It's crazy that people still breed animals for sale in pet shops when there are so many homeless and unwanted creatures in shelters and rescue centres.

Exotic pets

Millions of 'exotic' animals, such as parrots, turtles, snakes, tropical fish, spiders and monkeys, are caught in

---

RSPCA statistics

Homes found, treatments and humane destructions, 1997

Homes found	Dogs	Cats	Misc	Totals
Headquarters establishments	4,730	7,246	4,540	16,516
Inspectors	336	1,256	1,787	3,379
Branch and branch establishments	22,794	34,201	11,326	68,321
Total	**27,860**	**42,703**	**17,653**	**88,216**

Treatments	Out-patients	First Aid	Operations	Totals
Veterinary vouchers and other assisted schemes	28,334	–	–	28,334
Headquarters establishments (excluding hospitals)	21,523	679	1,119	23,321
Hospitals	117,127	11,258	28,400	156,785
Branch establishments	64,059	–	–	64,059
Total	**231,043**	**11,937**	**29,519**	**272,499**

Humane destructions*	Dogs	Cats	Misc	Totals
Headquarters establishments (excluding hospitals)	97	164	–	261
Branch establishments (inc vouchers)	725	1,632	253	2,610
Total	**822**	**1,796**	**253**	**2,871**

Humane destructions of animals for medical reasons	Dogs	Cats	Misc	Totals
Headquarters establishments (excluding hospitals)	760	978	2,373	4,111
Hospitals	3,678	4,053	3,775	11,515
Inspectors	1,578	9,312	35,353	46,243
Branch establishments (inc vouchers)	9,349	7,704	8,944	22,997
Total	12,635	22,056	50,445**	84,866

* Such destructions only occur with great reluctance when there is no reasonable possibility of rehoming. The Society is opposed to long-term confinement of animals which cannot be rehomed as this can cause distress and suffering to the animal concerned. This figure also includes animals destroyed at the owner's request.
** This igure includes wild birds and small wild mammals such as rabbits and hedgehogs. It also includes orphan animals too young to rear or too severely injured for return to the wild.

Source: RSPCA

the wild and imported into this country for people to keep as pets.

These animals are becoming increasingly popular, despite the fact that they need specialist food and living conditions and are, therefore, difficult to look after.

In 1991, over 129,000 parrots and other exotic birds were imported into Britain. More than 19,000 died within the first few weeks of arriving. It is thought that only one in four survive the ordeal of being captured in the wild, packed into crates and transported to pet shops around the world. This means that nearly 400,000 birds died *before* reaching the UK. This cruel trade is one reason why many species of birds and animals are becoming rare in the wild.

Sadly, the RSPCA report that most parrots who survive the terrible journey will die from disease, stress or injury within the first year. In the wild, a parrot's life expectancy is about 50 years. In captivity they are unlikely to live beyond five years. Birds should not be kept as pets. Parrots and budgerigars are highly intelligent, social animals who live in large flocks. But as pets they are often kept in solitary confinement. They prefer to spend their time flying around, preening their partner or foraging for food, but kept in cages they cannot do any of these things. Just imagine how much these poor creatures must suffer when they are captured, loaded into crates and then forced to live alone for the rest of their lives.

Large numbers of other 'exotic' animals will also die during capture and transportation, or will have short and unhappy lives as pets because their owners don't know how to look after them properly.

What can be done?

The government could do more to control and regulate the pet trade. Banning the importation of exotic wild animals such as parrots and stopping the sale of animals in pet shops would be a start. It could also help to set up more neutering and spaying schemes for cats and dogs and introduce controls on breeders to restrict the numbers and kinds of animals they breed. Much could also be done to educate people and teach them about responsible pet owner-ship.

Designer pets

Centuries of selective breeding have changed the look and nature of our pet animals, shortening and lengthening their bodies, legs and hair without any regard for their welfare. Humans have bred bulldogs and Pekinese dogs who wheeze and puff as they struggle to breathe through their squashed noses, chihuahuas who are so small they suffer from fragile bones, and rottweilers who are bred to be so aggressive they can be dangerous.

The demand for ever more bizarre and unusual pets has meant some animals have been turned into freaks. The sharpei dog has skin which hangs in folds because it is far too big for its body.

Cats have been bred without fur and rabbits with ears so long they can't walk properly. Some dogs are not considered 'proper' examples of their breed unless they have their tails removed or 'docked'. Many vets now refuse to carry out this cruel operation on puppies.

Paws for thought

Many people keep animals like rabbits, mice, birds and fish in cages and tanks. Some of these animals are captured in the wild while others are bred in this country. Even if they are well cared for, do you think they can be really happy?

What about their natural instincts to burrow, live with others of their own kind, forage or fly?

Do you think it is right to keep pets in such confined spaces?

Guidelines

Animals can be very loving and loyal friends. But we should not take them for granted. It doesn't matter if your pet is a large horse or a tiny goldfish – all animals have individual needs: a proper home, space, correct diet, constant water supply, exercise, companionship, opportunities for play and privacy, and also mental stimulation.

There are lots of things you will need to think about before you take on responsibility for an animal who will be totally dependent on you for the rest of his or her life.

- READ up as much information as you can about the animal you want before you bring it home.

- DON'T buy an animal that has been captured from the wild or imported from another country.

- DON'T buy animals from a pet shop or a breeder. (Instead, give a home to an animal from a sanctuary or rescue centre.)

- DON'T allow your pet to breed. Have your cat or dog neutered or spayed to avoid adding to the pet population.

Questions to ask yourself:

- Why do you want a pet? Can you offer him or her a good home for life?

- Have you considered carefully all his or her needs? (For example, dogs cannot be left alone all day.)
- Can you afford to feed your pet and pay vet bills? Who will look after him or her when you are away?
- Do you *really* have time to look after your pet properly?
- Will he or she need a companion? (Nearly all animals do. Hamsters are one of the few who need to live alone.)

© *Animal Aid*

The puppy farms that breed misery

Rory Carroll on MP's battle to halt illegal trade in 'battery dogs'

Hunched inside his pet shop cage, rheumy eyes peering through the bars, the puppy looks the embodiment of loneliness and innocence. He is neither of these things.

Rewind six weeks and watch as he is born in a converted cowshed teeming with dozens of diseased, yelping newborn dogs, all entering the same multi-million pound industry of the puppy farms.

Factories would be a better word, for the puppies are products, bought and sold for profit, exported and made to order.

Credit card in hand, you can phone your nearest dial-a-dog dealer, express your preference and wait for delivery, just like pizza.

You may not get what you pay for. Pneumonia, pleurisy, diarrhoea, worms, vomiting blood, skeletal deformations and huge vets' bills are not part of the deal but can come price included.

Dissatisfied customers have the option of returning their purchases and seeking a refund, but those who try usually falter when they see the conditions to which the puppy is returning.

According to the RSPCA breeding farms are often cramped, dirty, dark and rife with sickness. Hereditary diseases are passed on by exhausted bitches which, like battery hens, are mated as often as possible, producing two or even three litters a year. Some are held down by pitchforks to be forcibly mated.

This week Mike Hall, Labour MP for Weaver Vale, published a private member's bill to shut illegal puppy farms and improve welfare standards of registered commercial breeders. Mr Hall's Breeding and Sale of Dogs Bill would also outlaw the sale of puppies to pet shops and unscrupulous dealers.

Like the anti-hunting issue, Labour promised such a measure if it was elected, and like the anti-hunting bill, the Breeding and Sale of Dogs Bill is likely to fail because the Government will not give it parliamentary time.

So it is business as usual this Christmas and indefinitely for the hundreds – no one knows how many – of puppy farms dotted all over Britain. Under the Breeding Dog Acts 1973 and 1991 farms with two or more breeding bitches are supposed to obtain a licence from the local authority. Many do not.

Nor does the licence guarantee good care since the yearly inspections are carried out by planning officers concerned with structural surroundings, not vets checking the dogs' welfare.

Three Welsh areas alone – Carmarthenshire, Ceredigion and Pembrokeshire – have 260 licensed breeders, with unlicensed breeders probably doubling that figure, according to the RSPCA.

Previous estimates that about 70,000 farmed puppies are bred and sold each year are well off the mark, says the Kennel Club. Noting that the 6.9 million dog population remains stable, the club has just produced a new estimate based on the number of dogs which must be coming on the market each year to replace those that die.

'We registered 273,341 puppies last year but demand is colossal and I'd say there were another 420,000 that weren't registered,' said a club spokesman, Brian Leonard.

Even allowing for privately bred pets that suggests an industry, assuming the average price of a pedigree puppy to be £250, worth upwards of £80 million.

Little if any of that money is used to improve the conditions in which the animals live, says A.J.M. Robson, a vet who has inspected dozens of licensed and unlicensed breeders.

Bizarrely, puppy farms are reported to have been the brainchild of the Department of Agriculture. Animal welfare groups say that in 1982 government advisers urged Welsh dairy farmers to breed dogs as a way of supplementing income hurt

by dwindling milk quotas. The department was unable to confirm or deny the allegation.

True or not, the industry is now clustered in south and west Wales and provides the main source of income for many farmers turned breeders.

Nick Southall, a veteran of raids for the National Canine Defence League, says: 'They've become extremely suspicious and won't allow people in to look, which isn't surprising when you see what's inside.'

Instead breeders go to the buyer, transporting puppies hundreds of miles in vans or car boots to half-way meeting points such as motorway service stations. The buyer, who typically obtained the breeder's phone number from a classified advert in a local newspaper, may also get the dog delivered to the doorstep.

Alternatively the public can buy from middlemen or pet shops, which in some ways is worse, argues the RSPCA, because it delays the vital socialisation puppies need to adapt to domestic life.

Prices this week at one pet shop in South London ranged from £275 for a King Charles Spaniel to £350 for a Staffordshire Bull Terrier. Prices included vaccination, six weeks' insurance and a breeding certificate, assured the salesman, who refused access to the backroom full of yelping sounds but provided for inspection a subdued eight-week-old Westland Terrier 'all the way from Wales'.

Not good enough, says the RSPCA. The only way to ensure a puppy has been bred properly is to see it with his or her mother. Difficult enough with the mother in Wales and the buyer in London, impossible when the buyer is in Japan, Taiwan and Hong Kong, where increasing numbers of puppies are flown, changing hands for more than £1,000.

Bored and fashion-conscious owners will sometimes trade them in, with restaurants known to snap up a dish appreciated by Chinese customers. A grim twist, says one animal welfare officer: 'A puppy is for life, not just Christmas dinner.'

Big rise in cases of animal abuse and neglect

By Kate Watson-Smyth

Cruelty to animals rose by 16 per cent last year with more than 2,000 recorded cases of animals suffering abuse and neglect, it was announced yesterday.

The Royal Society for the Prevention of Cruelty to Animals said that despite its efforts to educate the public about responsible pet care, the number of convictions for animal cruelty rose from 2,282 in 1996 to 2,650 last year.

Cats and dogs are the most common victims, but cruelty to wildlife almost doubled in 1997, rising from 121 cases in 1996 to 221 last year.

Richard Davies, the RSPCA's chief officer of inspectorate, said: 'While public donations allow us to bring the perpetrators of cruelty to justice, it's the many animals that suffer at the hands of cruel owners who pay the ultimate price.

'It is incredibly frustrating for RSPCA inspectors, who work so hard to prevent cruelty, to continue to see an increase in the number of animals found abused and living in appalling conditions.'

The number of calls to the society's hotline reporting emergencies and seeking advice rose by more than 7 per cent from 1,303,481 in 1996 to 1,397,516 last year, amounting to one call every 22 seconds. And the number of defendants prosecuted by the RSPCA rose by 23 per cent, from 971 in 1996 to 1,195 in 1997.

Alex Ross, a spokesman for the society, said: 'It is very worrying that although there are more and more television programmes trying to educate people about responsible pet ownership, the numbers are still going up. People seem to forget that a cat or a dog lives for about 10 years which is longer than most people

A total of 8,255 animals were rescued from danger and 169,846 unwanted, sick and injured animals were collected

will own their car and they need to think about that when they get a pet.'

However, the figures also show that a total of 8,255 animals were rescued from danger and 169,846 unwanted, sick and injured animals were collected. The highest number of convictions was in the North-east with 570, compared with 96 in the South-west.

The Tory MP Roger Gale, chairman of the all-party Parliamentary Welfare Group, said people who are cruel to animals should face a lifetime ban on owning them.

'While I am, of course, pleased that RSPCA inspectors are bringing the abusers to court, the fact remains that there are still some courts that are not prepared to throw the book at the perpetrator and ban them from owning animals – for life if necessary. For the kind of people that we are talking about, a fine and costs is likely to prove no real deterrent and the magistrates' courts must recognise that when passing sentence,' he said.

Animal smuggling is the most lucrative crime after drugs

By Ian Burrell, Home Affairs Correspondent

The illegal trafficking of exotic and endangered species is now the biggest international criminal activity after the drugs trade, according to Interpol.

A senior officer said yesterday that the growing illicit market for rare animals and plants was worth £4bn a year. Some of the most sought-after species are being sold illegally through British pet sops.

Paul Andrews, environmental crime specialist at Interpol, which is based at the National Criminal Intelligence Service, said: 'Britain is one of the major purchasing countries for these rare species and we have criminals here brokering sales for the markets in America and Japan.'

British species are also being targeted. Dutch and German police have warned that organised gangs of traders in birds of prey are taking carefully planned trips to Scotland to raid the nests of golden eagles, red kites and peregrine falcons. The Royal Society for the Protection of Birds said last night that there had been a marked increase in such thefts, with 40 peregrine falcons stolen last year. The world's most wanted rare bird is the Lear's macaw, of which only 98 are believed to still exist.

Three of the birds – which are worth around £80,000 each – were found in raids on houses in Yorkshire in April. It is believed they were brought to Britain from Australia, South America and Malaysia.

During the raids, Customs officers also seized 10 palm cockatoos and several yellow-tailed and red-tailed black cockatoos, both endangered species, and worth up to £10,000.

One of the most frequently smuggled exotic birds is the hyacinth macaw, which will fetch around £20,000. The traders estimate that they need to smuggle 12 eggs to have a good chance of one surviving.

Many of the bird smugglers wear customised jackets beneath their outer clothing. Each jacket contains up to 20 pouches in which the rare eggs are placed in the knowledge that they will not show up on X-ray machines.

> ## One of the most frequently smuggled exotic birds is the hyacinth macaw, which will fetch around £20,000

The illegal trade in tortoises is also buoyant. Customs officers at Dover and Heathrow airport have seized India Star tortoises, which are usually smuggled in hand luggage and can be worth £1,000 each.

The RSPB said last night that German falconers were believed to be mainly responsible for the loss of 40 peregrine falcons reported stolen last year. There are only 1,300 pairs in the UK.

Guy Shorrock, investigations officer for the RSPB, said: 'During the last two breeding seasons there seems to have been a renewed interest in our native peregrines, particularly the ones from Scotland. There are a lot of indications that a number of birds are being taken and laundered on the Continent, especially in Germany.'

The thieves often come in camper vans, equipped with incubators run from the vehicle's generator. They take the birds back to the Continent and pass them off as captive-bred.

Mr Shorrock said that the internal UK market for peregrines had almost died out following the prosecution of several dealers through DNA testing of the birds.

But falconry is highly popular in Germany, where dealers also have

THEY WERE SO BUSY LOOKING FOR DRUGS THAT THEY MISSED THE SNOW LEOPARD!

KenPyne

contacts with Arab falconers prepared to pay thousands of pounds for wild-bred birds. He said: 'German and Dutch falconers are coming over to Britain themselves but there are a number of people here who are willing to help for money.' Two men from the Netherlands are facing charges in relation to alleged attempts to buy peregrine falcons in contravention of the Convention on International Trade in Endangered Species.

Later this year Interpol is due to publish a report on the international trade in primates based on a world-wide police survey of reported thefts and seizures.

The rarest of the rare: the most prized targets for animal smugglers

Gila monster
What are they?
Venomous lizard about 50cm long. Stout-bodied with black and pink blotches or bands and beadlike scales. Feeds on small mammals, birds and eggs.
Original habitat
Named after the Gila River Basin in America, it is found in the south-western United States and northern Mexico.
Rarity
Rare, it is one of only two species of venomous lizards.
Value
Well over £1,000 each.
Who buys them and why?
The reptile trade is one of the fastest growing sectors of the pet industry and the Gila Monster is now highly-fashionable, particularly among London collectors.

Indian star tortoise
What are they?
Its shell is covered in a lattice of yellow radiating lines which form an almost perfect camouflage. Up to 28cm in shell length, it feeds upon leaves, flowers and fallen fruits.
Original habitat
Sri Lanka and peninsular India. A typical clutch comprises seven eggs which take 150 days or more to incubate.
Rarity
Endangered but now being bred in captivity in increasing numbers.

Juveniles are at high risk from predators and increased mechanisation of agriculture is reducing their habitat.
Value
£1,000 each.
Who buys them and why?
Huge demand among collectors, many of whom may not realise trade is illegal. Sometimes unwittingly sold in pet shops.

Peregrine falcon
What are they?
Also called a Duck Hawk. Blue-grey with white underparts. It flies high and dives at tremendous speed, striking with clenched talons and killing on impact.
Original habitat
Found in Scotland and once plentiful in North America. Nests on high ledges or cliffs in open rocky country near water where birds are plentiful.
Rarity
There are 1,300 pairs left in the UK. Extinct in the eastern United States and endangered elsewhere in America.
Value
£800. Double if sold in Continental Europe. Price goes up even more if sold to falconers in Middle East.
Who buys them and why?
Sold to falconers, especially in Germany and Holland. They are sometimes used to breed hybrid

falcons because 'well-bred' pedigree is highly sought-after. Exceptional birds will be sold to Arab falconers.

Lear's macaw
What are they?
Deep-blue, with wings and back in a contrasting richer blue. Has a wing span of up to 42 inches. Also known as the Indigo Macaw.
Original habitat
Dry limestone landscapes in the Pernambuco and Bahia regions of north-eastern Brazil.
Rarity
Rarest of all parrots, it was thought to be extinct. The first proven field observations did not occur until 1978. The areas where the 98 remaining birds are found are extremely remote and hardly explored even now.
Value
£80,000 each.
Who buys them and why?
Collectors know that any dealings in these birds are illegal. The most prized bird in the illegal trade in parrots. Three were seized this year during Customs raids in Yorkshire.

Hyacinth macaw
What are they?
Stunning cobalt-blue plumage and black bill. Regarded as the 'King of all parrot-like birds'. Lives off fruit and nuts, especially of palm trees.
Original habitat
Lives in the riverside areas of Savannah-forest countries. Most common in the South-Central area of Brazil, it is found as far as the borders with Bolivia and Paraguay.
Rarity
Extremely rare, it has 'red list' status under international rules in the trade of rare species. It is described as 'vulnerable and rare' in all three of its habitat countries, Brazil, Paraguay and Bolivia.
Value
£20,000 or £50,000 for a breeding pair.
Who buys them and why?
Sold to collectors. The most widely available of the Macaws sold on the illegal market. Traders estimate they need to smuggle a dozen eggs for one to survive.

The killing season

The annual seal hunt has just started. The Canadian government says that it is the only way to restore fish stocks. The rest of the world is not so sure. John Crace investigates

Lovability is a prime asset in the animal world. And seals have more than their fair share. Indeed, it was photographs of appealing, defenceless white seal pups lying on the ice in a pool of blood that were primarily responsible for the European Union banning the import of Canadian harp and hooded seal skins in 1983. This, in turn, led to the Canadian government forbidding the commercial slaughter of baby whitecoat harp seals in 1989.

But the lovability factor has not been enough to save hundreds of thousands of seals every year. Throughout the 1990s the Canadian government has steadily been increasing the seal kill quota. This year the quota has been set at a record level of 275,000 harp seals and 10,000 hooded seals.

Moreover, many of those killed will be pups under one year old. The Canadian ban on baby seals only extends to those under 12 days old. Any other seal is regarded as fair game.

The annual seal cull is the largest marine mammal hunt in the world. It is therefore the subject of much controversy. Those in favour say it is an economic and ecological necessity. Those against say these arguments are fundamentally flawed, and that the killing is nothing but an inhumane waste of time, energy and life.

Economics

For centuries the Inuit have depended on seal blubber, meat and fur for fuel, food and clothing. But the recent increases in Canadian seal quota have nothing to do with the Inuit, and everything to do with the collapse of the Newfoundland fishing industry.

In 1992, the Grand Banks fishery, the region's major employer, was shut down after the

cod stocks were destroyed by overfishing. According to the environmental pressure group, IFAW (International Fund for Animal Welfare), despite the fact that 25 out of 27 independent scientists found otherwise, the Canadian government chose to blame the decline in cod stocks on rising seal numbers and decided to increase the kill quotas.

Under ordinary circumstances, no one would have bothered to take up the government's offer. The Norwegian factory ships, which had previously taken most of the seal carcasses, had been evicted from Canadian waters in 1987, and the price of the pelts had fallen from C$40 (£20) to C$9. In short, it simply wasn't financially worthwhile to hunt seals and, by 1993, the cull had reached a low of 27,000.

So, faced with 30,000 newly unemployed fishermen with no obvious hope of finding work, the Canadian government opted to boost the sealing industry by artificially raising the price of seal products. This was done by paying subsidies. In 1996, C$1.6 million was paid out in seal meat subsidies.

Even so, a recent study shows that the annual hunt provides the equivalent of 100-120 full-time jobs, just 0.06 per cent of Newfoundland's total workforce.

Around the world

Although the largest hunt takes place in Canada, seals are killed all over the world.

Britain: Seal hunting is banned in this country. Even so there have been isolated incidents. In May 1996, seven seals were found clubbed and slashed to death on holiday beaches in north Yorkshire. Suspicion focused on local fishermen who blamed the seals for taking salmon and sea-trout from their nets. Early last year, eight seals were found dead in the Shetland islands. Again, fishermen were blamed.

Namibia: The Cape Cross fur-seal population off Namibia's Skeleton Coast suffered devastating losses in 1994 after fish migrated away from their feeding grounds. Even so, the Namibian government has failed to stop the annual hunt. IFAW claims that with 30 per cent unemployment, Namibia is trying to breathe life into a dying industry.

Norway: Seal hunting is restricted to harp and hooded seals over one year old. Annual catch quotas are set on the basis of scientific recommendations from the International Council for the Exploration of the Sea and the Norwegian Institute of Marine Research. They believe that if the population becomes too large, then seals will migrate close to the coast in search of food, thereby threatening fish stocks.

Russia: Even though the seal population of the White Sea ice-fields off Murmansk and Archangel is in desperate decline, the Russian government refuses to end its annual 10-day cull, because to do so would threaten jobs. Environmentalists say that the fur farms cannot sell the pelts because Russian consumers prefer foreign imports. However, the government is determined to continue sealing no matter how unprofitable it becomes.

The 1996 Canadian hunt

Facts and figures: a study by IFAW of the cull two years ago revealed the full horror of the seal slaughter.

Sealers took three times the legal limit for hooded seals. Overall, 500,000 (or twice the annual quota) were killed during the hunt. This estimate is due to the large number that are wounded but never recovered or counted in official statistics.

Sealers should make sure that all animals are dead by touching each seal's eye and watching for a 'blinking reflex'. Few bothered to administer this simple test.

101 sealers, including the President and one-third of the Executive Council of the Canadian Sealers' Association, were charged with selling more than 25,000 protected whitecoat harp and blueback hooded seal pups for profit.

Film evidence shows that sealers often shoot as many animals as possible and then go back to finish off the wounded. This causes tremendous suffering for the seals that are left to bleed to death.

The killing is done in two ways. Adults are shot with a rifle, while a club or 'hakapik' is used on the young. The hakapik may also be used on adults which have been shot to ensure they are dead. Sealers claim that though the hakapik looks primitive, it is an extremely effective tool.

One sealer was convicted of skinning a seal alive after the International Fund for Animal Welfare (IFAW) provided video-taped documentary evidence.

Observers found evidence of the widespread dumping of seal skins and bodies. Such waste is characteristic of the hunt.

Sealers are supposed to bleed animals after killing to ensure the animal is dead and protect the meat from spoilage. Video evidence suggests that sealers often skip this step in the rush to kill as many animals as possible.

Other filmed footage shows sealers using sharpened steel hooks to catch seals and drag them on board. This practice allows the sealers to work faster but is illegal as it causes tremendous suffering for animals that are still alive.

Seals are not meant to be shot while swimming, as a clean kill cannot be guaranteed. Nevertheless, the practice is quite common.

Sealers routinely kill pregnant females in January and February – just weeks before they give birth. Near full-term foetuses are sometimes stuffed and mounted as souvenirs of the kill.

Local hoteliers in Newfoundland complained that the stench of rotting seals was damaging their business.

The penis is by far the most valuable part of the seal. Numerous abandoned corpses, with their penises removed, were found both on the ice and in the water.

Dividing the spoils

The Canadian government has launched a slick marketing campaign to highlight the different beneficial uses for seal products in order to dispel the idea that the seal corpses are wasted. Even so, the public are far from convinced and were it not for government subsidies, sealing would not be commercially viable. As it is, a large percentage of the seals that are killed are dumped on the ice.

Enzymes: seal enzymes can be used to make Cheddar cheese.

Fur: may be used for clothing.

Skin: may be used as a substitute for leather.

Powdered meat: this can be used as a protein supplement.

Meat: the back is supposed to be the tastiest and most tender cut. Marketers have been trying to promote seal pepperoni as a pizza topping.

Seal-oil: Canadian health stores are selling capsules of seal-oil, which is a rich source of Omega-3 fatty acids, as an antidote to many illnesses, such as diabetes and arthritis.

Seal skin cream: supposedly alleviates dry, itchy symptoms

Penis: ground up genitals are highly valued as an aphrodisiac in the Far East. The illegal export of seal penises is alleged to be widespread in Canada.

© *The Independent*
May, 1998

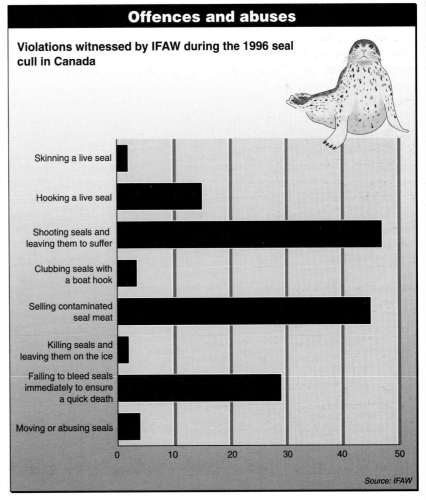

Offences and abuses

Violations witnessed by IFAW during the 1996 seal cull in Canada

- Skinning a live seal
- Hooking a live seal
- Shooting seals and leaving them to suffer
- Clubbing seals with a boat hook
- Selling contaminated seal meat
- Killing seals and leaving them on the ice
- Failing to bleed seals immediately to ensure a quick death
- Moving or abusing seals

0   10   20   30   40   50

Source: IFAW

Wildlife crime

Information from the Metropolitan Police

Many people think, quite wrongly, that because London is mainly urban, it does not suffer from wildlife crime. The Metropolitan Police District includes parts of Kent, Surrey, Hertfordshire and Essex which are country areas with large populations of wild animals, birds and plants, many of which are protected by law.

At the same time many animals and birds have adapted very successfully to living in the city. Foxes, kestrels and muntjac deer, for instance, are an increasingly common sight in London today.

The amount of wildlife crime investigated in London is reflected by our very large human population. For example, the Londoner who takes birds or their eggs from the wild may not find them in London but once he/she returns home it becomes a Metropolitan Police matter. From this you can see that our involvement in wildlife matters can actually be greater than for some police forces in more rural areas.

What is wildlife crime?

Wildlife crime takes many forms, from people shooting at birds with air guns in the local park to the more organised crimes of badger baiting and the trade in endangered species.

Some of the following are crimes which we come up against in the London area:

Badger crime

Although badgers are perceived to be one of Britain's best-loved animals, the sad truth is that they have been persecuted by man for centuries. Shy creatures, they avoid contact with people and are seldom seen, living in underground setts and only emerging at night to feed. London and its surrounding countryside has its own badger population so crime against this animal is very much a concern of the Metropolitan Police Service.

Because they are nocturnal animals, they are particularly vulnerable to disturbance in their setts during the day, Recent years have seen an upsurge in the old practices of badger digging and baiting.

Badger baiting is a crime

Badger diggers use dogs and spades to get badgers from their setts. The captured badgers are then attacked by dogs for 'sport'. Even if the badger survives the attack, it is likely to have suffered severe injuries and will ultimately be killed by the diggers. The dogs often receive serious injuries as well.

Badger baiting, like cock fighting, used to be a popular spectator sport. It was made illegal in 1835 but probably never died out in some country areas and has become more common in the last 20 years or so. It

is a highly organised contest, usually held away from the sett, sometimes in towns and cities like London. At a baiting event spectators bet on the performance of the dogs against the badger, which is often disabled in some way before the baiting to give the dogs a better chance. In some parts of the country the badger population has been almost destroyed by the activities of diggers and baiters.

Badgers and the law

All badgers and their setts are fully protected in the law under The Protection of Badgers Act 1992. Anyone who takes, kills, or injures a badger, or who interferes with a badger sett, can be sent to prison for six months or fined up to £5,000.

What can you do to protect badgers?

Badger groups play a vital role in protecting badgers. They are made up of volunteers who work with the police and the RSPCA to enforce the laws protecting badgers. In some areas they have even built artificial setts that are 'digger proof'. If you would like to join your local group, please contact

The National Federation of Badger Groups, 15 Cloisters Business Centre, 8 Battersea Park Road, London, SW8 4BG

If you see people with digging equipment and dogs in an area where

badgers live, do not approach them but note down the registration number of any cars parked nearby and telephone the police immediately.

Remember – when people kill or maim badgers they are committing a crime as well as destroying the wildlife in your area.

Bird crime

Birds are part of our lives, and whether we live in town or the country there are few of us who do not see them every day.

All British birds, their nests and eggs are protected by law, and yet the Royal Society for the Protection of Birds receives reports of over 1,000 offences committed against birds in Britain every year. Many others go unreported. The London area is home to many different species of wild birds, from garden song birds to wildfowl on the lakes and rivers, and some rare birds of prey. It is also home to around 8 million people. Unfortunately, some of these travel extensively committing crimes against birds, both in this country and abroad, and the Metropolitan Police Wildlife Officers are often required to investigate these offences.

Wild birds and the law

All British birds, their nests and eggs are protected under The Wildlife and Countryside Act 1981. Anyone found guilty of an offence may be fined up to £1,000. Some rarer species are specially protected and in these cases offenders may be fined up to £5,000.

In law it is also an offence to attempt to commit an offence against wild birds.

Typical crimes against birds
Illegal persecution
Many birds each year are shot, poisoned or illegally trapped. Even such popular birds as swans and herons are persecuted and become victims of cruelty.

Egg collecting
Egg collecting has been illegal since 1954 yet some collectors persist in their activities, and some very large collections have been seized by police in recent years.

Taking birds from the wild
In the London area many small song birds, like goldfinches, are trapped illegally to supply the cage bird market. Some rare birds of prey like peregrine falcons and goshawks also turn up here having been taken from the wild in other parts of the UK for the falconry market.

The keeping of birds is legal, provided that they have been bred in captivity. In the case of some rarer species, the keeper must register the bird with the Department of the Environment.

In recent years Metropolitan Police Wildlife Officers have recovered many rare birds of prey which were taken from the wild illegally, and collections of birds' eggs, as well as finch trapping equipment, and have dealt with many cases of birds being killed illegally.

Scientific advances have enabled the police to use increasingly sophisticated techniques in the detection of crime. In a recent case involving a large number of peregrine falcons taken from the wild illegally the Metropolitan Police used DNA testing to prove that the birds had not been captive-bred.

It is an offence to deliberately release any species of bird which does not normally live wild in this country. This also applies to captive-bred barn owls which cannot be released without a Department of the Environment licence.

How you can help protect wild birds
The Royal Society for the Protection of Birds (RSPB), with nearly one million members, is the largest conservation organisation protecting birds in Britain. The RSPB owns and manages many nature reserves throughout the country and has a number of local members' groups in the London area.

RSPB officers work closely with police wildlife officers and provide expert advice and assistance in cases of bird crime. If you want to know more about the laws protecting birds in Britain, the RSPB publishes a more detailed guide, *Wild Birds and the Law*.

For more information please write to: RSPB, The Lodge, Sandy, Bedford-shire, SG19 2DL

The Metropolitan Police is committed to enforcing the laws protecting wild birds.

If you know of anybody who is committing crimes against birds or any other wildlife, please call Crimestoppers on 0800 555 111. Your call is free. You don't have to give your name and you could earn a cash reward.

Protecting wildlife – the police response
All British police forces have appointed a specialist Wildlife Liaison Officer (WLO) to take the lead in enforcing the laws protecting our wildlife. The Metropolitan Police WLO is based at New Scotland Yard from where he co-ordinates and supports the work of the Met's Area Wildlife Officers. He also maintains contact with many conservation organisations, local badger groups, government departments, other police forces and individuals involved in wildlife protection as well as acting as a focal point for information and enquiries from the public. Wildlife Liaison Officers are police officers who have been specially selected for their interest in, and knowledge of, wildlife matters.

In addition, Metropolitan Police Wildlife Officers deal with many other aspects of wildlife crime including the illegal trade in endangered species of exotic birds such as parrots.

© *Directorate of Public Affairs and Internal Communication, Metropolitan Police Service November, 1998*

Britain leads fight against the cruel zoos

By Greg Neale, Environment Correspondent

Britain is to lead a campaign against Europe's cruel zoos. Ministers hope that moves tomorrow will end the keeping of wild animals in cramped, sterile cages or pens, often with poor husbandry and inadequate veterinary care.

Michael Meacher, the Environment Minister, will use Britain's presidency of the European Union to urge his continental colleagues to adopt a zoos directive – the first such regulation to cover the entire EU.

Ministers at the EU Environment Council will discuss moves contained in the directive to establish minimum levels of animal husbandry and care throughout all licensed zoos in Europe. At present, only a few countries – including Britain, Germany, Holland, Sweden and Finland – have enforced standards for animal welfare in zoos.

Mr Meacher said yesterday: 'This is an issue which Britain and the British people take seriously. The directive would encourage the conservation work of zoos, as well as put into place rules for licensing and inspecting them.'

He added: 'These [animals] are living creatures which I believe have a right to proper care and conditions. At present, there is evidence of poor standards at too many zoos in Europe.'

Bill Travers, of the animal charity the Born Free Foundation, yesterday welcomed the move. 'The majority of European zoos fall below an acceptable standard, and would certainly require improvements to meet British legal standards.' Among examples found by Mr Travers and his colleagues in a survey of European zoos were:

- An elephant in Spain with an untreated wound 'as big as a chopping board'.
- Old and infirm animals alive and on show 'even though they were so debilitated that a modern, veterinary decision would be to have them humanely put down'.
- Polar bears and big cats kept in small cages or enclosures, with insufficient interest, so that their behaviour becomes increasingly psychotic and stereotypical – the

> *At present, only a few countries – including Britain, Germany, Holland, Sweden and Finland – have enforced standards for animal welfare in zoos*

animals pace incessantly in their confinement.

- Animals such as deer and antelopes kept on soft ground, with no hard standing or regular veterinary care to trim their hooves.

'Untended hooves just grow and curl over, leaving the animals crippled,' Mr Travers said. 'I've seen animals in Belgian zoos kept in sickening conditions – a lion that was so ill and decrepit it was being fed liquidised slop. In Greece, we found two lions being kept in an Athens aviary, with a simple concrete floor. When my father spoke to Greek authorities in the early Nineties, he was told there was no vet with exotic husbandry experience in the country and that zoos were simply not inspected. This is why we need this directive.'

A spokesman for the World Society for the Protection of Animals backed Mr Meacher's support for a new directive. 'We frequently receive complaints from the public about zoos they have visited in Europe,' he said.

While Mr Meacher chairs this week's meeting, Angela Eagle, a junior environment minister, will press Britain's support for the directive.

© *Telegraph Group Limited, London 1998*

ADDITIONAL RESOURCES

You might like to contact the following organisations for further information. Due to the increasing cost of postage, many organisations cannot respond to enquiries unless they receive a stamped, addressed envelope.

Advocates for Animals
10 Queensferry Street
Edinburgh, EH2 4PG
Tel: 0131 225 6039
Protects animals from cruelty and prevents the infliction of suffering. Produces a wide range of booklets on animal experiments and animal sports.

Animal Aid
The Old Chapel
Bradford Street
Tonbridge
Kent, TN9 1AW
Tel: 01732 364546
Fax: 01732 366533
Animal Aid aims to expose and campaign peacefully against the abuse of animals in all its forms and to promote a cruelty-free lifestyle. Produces information including their quarterly magazine *Outrage*. To receive information on an issue or for a list of educational and information resources, please send a large s.a.e. to the address above.

Animals in Medicines Research Information Centre (AMRIC)
The Association of the British Pharmaceutical Industry
12 Whitehall
London, SW1A 2DY
Tel: 0171 588 0841
Fax: 0171 747 1414
AMRIC was established by the pharmaceutical industry to provide information to the public about the essential role of laboratory animals in the discovery, development and safety-testing of medicines and vaccines.

Cosmetic, Toiletry & Perfumery Association (CTPA)
Josaron House
5-7 John Princes Street
London, W1M 9HD
Tel: 0171 491 8891
Fax: 0171 493 8061
Represents the cosmetics companies.

Countryside Alliance
The Old Town Hall
367 Kennington Road
London, SE11 4PT
Tel: 0171 582 5432
Fax: 0171 793 8899
Countryside Alliance defends field sports and organises rallies. It is comprised of the British Field Sports Society, the Countryside Movement, and the Countryside Business Group.

Hunt Saboteurs
PO Box 2786
Brighton, BN2 2AX
Tel: 01273 622 827
Strongly opposed to all blood sports.

International Fund for Animal Welfare (IFAW)
Warren Court, Park Road
Crowborough, TN6 2GA
Tel: 01892 601900
Fax: 01892 601926
IFAW was founded in 1969 and is one of the world's largest animal protection and conservation organisations.

League Against Cruel Sports (LACS)
83–87 Union Street
London, SE1 1SG
Tel: 0171 403 6155
Campaigns for a change in the legislation to give wildlife proper protection and outlaw hunting with dogs.

Metropolitan Police Service
Wildlife Liaison Officer
Room 913, New Scotland Yard
Broadway
London, SW1H 0BG
Tel: 0171 230 1212
Fax: 0171 230 4276
Maintains contact with many conservation organisations, government departments, other police forces and individuals involved in wildlife protection as well as acting as a focal point for information and enquiries from the public.

PETA (People for the Ethical Treatment of Animals)
PO Box 3169
London, SW15 3ZG
Tel: 0181 785 3113
Anti-experiments lobby group which targets animal abuse in laboratories, in the fur and meat trades, and in the entertainment industry. Produces a range of factsheets, leaflets and a free information pack on animal experiments.

Research Defence Society (RDS)
58 Great Marlborough Street
London, W1V 1DD
Fax: 0171 287 2818
Supports the responsible use of animals in medical and biological research. Leaflets, factsheets, videos and speakers available.

Royal Society for the Prevention of Cruelty to Animals (RSPCA)
The Causeway
Horsham
West Sussex, RH12 1HG
Tel: 01403 264181
Fax: 01403 241048
The RSPCA is a charity and the world's oldest animal welfare organisation. Whether it is lobbying for change in the parliaments of Westminster or Strasbourg, providing food, shelter and treatment for abandoned dogs and cats, tracking down dangerous dogfights or prosecuting animal abusers in the court, the Society can be found just about anywhere the welfare of animals is at stake

Wildlife Network
Mowbray Lodge
6 Catmos Street
Oakham
Rutland, LE15 6HW
Tel: 01572 771 355
Fax: 01572 771356
Wildlife Network is a wildlife conservation group. It seeks to find common ground between those for and against fox-hunting.

INDEX

The Internet has been likened to shopping in a supermarket without aisles. The press of a button on a Web browser can bring up thousands of sites but working your way through them to find what you want can involve long and frustrating on-line searches. And unfortunately many sites contain inaccurate, misleading or heavily biased information. Our researchers have therefore undertaken an extensive analysis to bring you a selection of quality Web site addresses.

* * * * *

Animal Aid
www.animalaid.org.uk
Provide educational materials and resources for secondary school students and teachers including student factsheets covering a wide range of issues.

World Animal Net
http://worldanimal.net
The world's largest database of animal protection societies, with over 6,000 listings and links to more than 1,500 web sites.

Countryside Alliance
www.countryside-alliance.org
In favour of field sports, this site provides information on shooting, falconry, hunting, stalking, angling, ferreting, coursing, conservation, lurcherwork and terrierwork.

League Against Cruel Sports (LACS)
www.league.uk.com
Has factsheets on hares and coursing, foxes and foxhunting.

Hunt Saboteurs Association
http://arrs.envirolink.org
Provides factsheets and articles which outline the views of the Hunt Saboteurs Association.

The Animal Rights Movement
http://arrs.envirolink.org
The Animal Rights Resource Site (ARRS) is a clearinghouse on the Internet for information related to the animal rights movement. Includes factsheets, essays and links to other relevant sites.

ACKNOWLEDGEMENTS

The publisher is grateful for permission to reproduce the following material.

While every care has been taken to trace and acknowledge copyright, the publisher tenders its apology for any accidental infringement or where copyright has proved untraceable. The publisher would be pleased to come to a suitable arrangement in any such case with the rightful owner.

Chapter One: Animal Research

Animal experimentation, © Christian Medical Fellowship (CMF), *Facts and figures on animal research in Great Britain*, © Research Defence Society, *How much research is done?*, © Research Defence Society, *What animals are used in research?*, © Research Defence Society, *Cosmetics and product testing*, © Animal Aid, *How many experiments?*, © Animal Aid, *The responsible way forward in bodycare*, © Cosmetic, Toiletry & Perfumery Association (CTPA), *A necessary evil?*, © Animal Aid, *Animal research*, © The Association of the British Pharmaceutical Industry (ABPI), *Primates in research & testing*, © RSPCA, *Animal welfare in the laboratory*, © Research Defence Society, *Animal rights*, © PETA.

Chapter Two: Hunting

Is hunting cruel?, © Countryside Alliance, *The facts about fox-hunting*, © RSPCA, *Country sports*, © Countryside Alliance, *Fox-hunting*, © Wildlife Network, August 1998, *Animal rights and wrongs*, ©

Telegraph Group Limited, London 1998, *This is foxhunting*, © Countryside Alliance 1998, *Hunting: focus on the figures*, © Countryside Alliance 1998, *Employment*, © Countryside Alliance 1998, *This is draghunting*, © Countryside Alliance 1998, *Draghunting – 'A family sport'*, © League Against Cruel Sports (LACS).

Chapter Three: Animal Cruelty

Companion animals, © Animal Aid, *RSPCA statistics*, © RSPCA, *The puppy farms that breed misery*, © The Guardian, December 1997, *Big rise in cases of animal abuse and neglect*, © The Independent, April 1998, *Animal smuggling is the most lucrative crime after drugs*, © The Independent, 1998, *The killing season*, © The Independent, May 1998, *Offences and abuses*, © IFAW, *Wildlife crime*, © Directorate of Public Affairs and Internal Communications, Metropolitan Police Service, *Britain leads fight against the cruel zoos*, © Telegraph Group Limited, London 19998.

Photographs and illustrations:

Pages 1, 9, 19, 32, 38: Pumpkin House, pages 2, 14, 21, 34, 40: Ken Pyne, page 17: Katherine Fleming.

Craig Donnellan
Cambridge
January, 1999